Fintan O'Toole was born in Dublin in 1958. He has been a columnist and critic with the *Irish Times* since 1988 and was drama critic of the *Daily News* in New York from 1997 until 2001. His books include *A Traitor's Kiss: The Life of Richard Brinsley Sheridan*, also published by Granta Books.

Shakespeare is Hard, but so is Life

*A Radical Guide to
Shakespearian Tragedy*

Fintan O'Toole

Granta Books
London · New York

Granta Publications, 2/3 Hanover Yard, Noel Road, London N1 8BE

First published in Great Britain, under the title *No More Heroes*,
by The Raven Arts Press 1990
This revised edition published by Granta Books 2002

1 3 5 7 9 10 8 6 4 2

Typeset in Baskerville by M Rules
Printed and bound in Great Britain by Mackays of Chatham plc

Contents

Editions of Shakespeare vary considerably. All references in this book are to *The Complete Works*, edited by Stanley Wells and Gary Taylor, published by Clarendon Press, Oxford, 1986. In the case of *King Lear*, Wells and Taylor give two different texts. Unless otherwise indicated, the references here are to the second version, based on the Folio of 1623.

To Clare, with love

1

Shakespeare is Hard, but so is Life

1. Muesli, Morals and a Bright Backside

The plays of William Shakespeare were written on the playing fields of Eton. Or, at least, the plays of Shakespeare as they have been taught in school, were. In the form in which most people first encounter them, *Hamlet* or *Macbeth*, *King Lear* or *Othello* are made to seem as if they have very little to do with the theatre, with the seventeenth century, with a man trying to create new rituals for a world that was changing at a frightening pace, and everything to do with building character, with the nineteenth century, with teaching us lessons about how we should behave. They are the mental equivalent of a cold shower; shocking, awful, but in some obscure way good for you, bracing you for the terrors of life and keeping your mind off bad thoughts about politics, society and the way the world changes. They are an ordeal after which you're supposed to feel better, a kind of mental muesli that cleans out the system and purges the soul. And, like muesli, they are boring, fruity and full of indigestible roughage.

The plays that Shakespeare actually wrote, on the other hand, are full of great stories, extraordinary people, wonderfully rich language and a skill with drama that has seldom been matched. They are not always easy, partly because the language of the sixteenth and seventeenth centuries, even when it appears to be the same as ours, can work very differently. When, for instance, Henry Vaughan in the seventeenth century writes 'How fair a prospect is a bright backside', he doesn't mean what you think he might mean; he's saying that it is nice to have a garden behind your house. And it works the other way too – Hamlet can sound like he's talking very respectably when in fact what he's saying is pure filth. So Shakespeare's language takes a bit of work. Shakespeare is hard, but so is life, and so long as you can see that there's a lot of life in Shakespeare, then the effort begins to make sense.

What doesn't make any sense is the idea that Shakespeare is trying to demonstrate moral ideas to us, that he's a kind of excruciatingly long-winded head nun. If you look at him this way, then he's not just boring and banal, he's also pretty stupid. One set of school notes on *Macbeth*, for instance, tells us that in 'moralistic terms, the Tragic hero and in particular Macbeth, may be seen as a warning to all that evil will be punished in this life as well as the next'. Leaving aside the fact that this is not a particularly startling thing to want to tell us, and that Shakespeare might have been better employed writing

2

sermons rather than plays if this was really what he wanted to do, we might well ask what moral message Shakespeare was trying to give us. The message of *Macbeth* is that it's a bad idea to kill kings. The message of *Hamlet* is that Hamlet should have killed the King sooner. Othello is doomed because he is too jealous of what he has. Lear is doomed because he is not jealous enough and wants to give away what he has. If this is what Shakespeare is about, then he's clearly not very good at it. Either there is something else entirely going on in his plays, or we should all go back to watching soap operas where at least the moral messages are fairly consistent.

2. Heroes, Greeks, Tragic Flaws and True Confessions

Before we can begin to understand, and therefore enjoy, Shakespeare's tragedies, there is a thick undergrowth to be cleared away: all that stuff about Tragic Heroes, Tragic Flaws, Fear and Pity, Character, and so on. Almost every school textbook on one of Shakespeare's tragedies starts out by showing that there is a thing called Tragedy which was defined by a man called Aristotle two and a half thousand years ago and that the play in question, *Hamlet*, *King Lear*, or whatever, conforms to this definition. The assumption seems to be that if for some reason the play did not do what Aristotle said a tragedy should do, then it would somehow cease to be any good and we wouldn't want to read it or see it. By a happy coincidence, the textbooks always find that there is no difficulty in showing that Shakespeare's plays were in fact written to Aristotle's formula, that they are therefore the real thing, and that it's okay to go ahead and study them.

The need for *Hamlet* or *Macbeth* or *Othello* or *King Lear* to be licensed by a Greek who died hundreds of years before the birth of Christ has very little to do with ancient Greece and still less to do with Elizabethan England. But it does have a lot to do with Victorian Britain, and with the critics and teachers of nineteenth-century England who laid down many of the categories through which most of us still encounter Shakespeare for the first time. Shakespeare himself may or may not have been aware of Aristotle's book, *The Poetics*, from which Italian and French scholars in the sixteenth and seventeenth centuries derived the rules of what a tragedy is supposed to be. While Aristotle was merely trying to describe what he thought the best writers of tragedy in his own time were doing, the courtly critics of the Renaissance turned these descriptions into a formula. In France, the formula became a prescription. In the England of Shakespeare's time it was largely ignored. We know very little about Shakespeare's life and very little about what he read, other than what he used for his plays. But even if he was familiar with the so-called Aristotelian rules, he felt free to ignore them. The strongest of these rules was the idea of the unities of time, place and action – the notion that tragedies should happen in a single day, in a single place and through a single story. Shakespeare's plays can take up to sixteen years to unfold, hop all over the place and usually involve more than one plot.

The only evidence of Shakespeare's attitude to Aristotle that we have from his plays is that he didn't know very much about him. Aristotle is mentioned twice in Shakespeare: once as having written before Homer, once as being the opposite to Ovid; references that are in one case wrong and in the other simply obscure. The most important of Aristotle's ideas about tragedy, 'catharsis' (the purging of the emotions), is never mentioned by Shakespeare and is referred to only once by any Elizabethan writer, and then only to mock at it. Even the word 'tragedy' itself is something that was forced on to Shakespeare's plays long after they were written. The Stationers' Register, which recorded the titles of his plays in Shakespeare's own time, lists *Hamlet* as a 'revenge', *King Lear* as a 'history', *Antony and Cleopatra* as 'a book called Antony and Cleopatra'. *Othello* is listed as a tragedy, but then so are *Richard II* and *Richard III*, which we now call 'history plays'.

When the plays were printed during Shakespeare's lifetime, their categorization as tragedies is even more dubious. *Hamlet* is a 'tragical history', *King Lear* is a 'true chronicle history'. Whatever else he was doing, Shakespeare was not sitting down to write something which was called 'tragedy' and which followed prescribed rules. He certainly knew that he was *not* writing the most respected and highbrow kind of tragedy of his day, the one which followed classical (mostly Roman) models.

The habit of seeing Shakespeare through Aristotle in fact has almost nothing at all to do with Shakespeare and is the invention of Victorian England. In the seventeenth and eighteenth centuries, both those who loved his work and those who didn't agreed that he didn't write classical tragedies. In 1692, the influential critic Thomas Rymer attacked Shakespeare for not being a proper tragedian, since he didn't follow the Aristotelian unities. (He called *Othello*, for example, a 'bloody farce'.) Thirty years later, an admirer, Alexander Pope, replied that 'to judge of Shakespear by Aristotle's rules is like trying a man by the Laws of one Country, who acted under those of another'.

The Victorians, however, were at the centre of a great world Empire and liked to think of themselves as the essence of modern civilization. Since they thought of ancient Greece as the essence of classical civilization, they naturally wanted to identify themselves with it as much as possible. If they could show that Shakespeare, a central part of their own culture, was really the first cousin once removed of their beloved Greeks, then Aristotle's ideas about tragedy would clean up Shakespeare, make him once and for all respectable, fit him in with their own taste for moral seriousness and good example.

Shakespeare was the missing link between the English public school and the sunlit heroism of ancient Greece, a notion nicely encapsulated in the remark of the Victorian politician and journalist Walter Bagehot – that from his school-ing Shakespeare had derived 'not exactly an acquaintance with Greek and Latin, but like Eton boys, a firm conviction that there are such languages'. Out of this combination of Eton and Athens, of Aristotle and soup-soap-and-salvation morality came the idea of the Tragic Flaw.

Victorian thinking about Shakespeare, much of which we have inherited, was dominated by Matthew Arnold's idea that literature had to be thought of as offering help to people who

were perplexed about how to live. Living in what they considered to be a stable and ordered society, the Victorian
intellectuals weren't much interested in those aspects of
Shakespeare (easily the most important ones) which are about
social and political change, about instability and its consequences. On the whole, they tended to view public affairs in
general with distaste, as something which made life crude and
corrupted its finer values. What interested them were the pecu-
liarities of Shakespeare's characters and the possibility which
they offered for some kind of moral guidance. They also
tended to regard the stories of Shakespeare's plays as out-
landish and far-fetched, as a crude concession to the populace,
saved only by the genius of Shakespeare's poetry. So they split
his characters from his stories and gave us the notion of looking at Shakespeare's characters in isolation from his plots, from
what is happening to them and around them. The main problem with this is that it makes much of what happens in
Shakespeare almost incomprehensible and almost all of it very
boring.

As well as reflecting their own view of the world, this idea of
what Shakespeare was about also reflected the Victorian theatre. Victorian theatre was dominated by great actor-managers
and by the picture-frame stage. Both of these contributed to
the idea of the star as the really important thing in the play.
So, for instance, *Othello* was about the actor playing Othello,
to a lesser extent the actor playing Iago, and a few hangers-on
to make up the numbers. Sir Walter Scott wrote at this time
that it was no longer the poetry or the plot which drew an
audience to *Hamlet* but the desire to compare some turn of

gesture or intonation in Kemble's performance with that of Garrick. This gave a great impetus to the isolated study of the Tragic Hero and, furthermore, to solitary moments in the tragedies, to the big scenes and particularly the soliloquies which were the testing ground of great heroic acting. Good modern productions of Shakespeare have long since moved on from this way of playing Shakespeare and towards the idea that, as the director Peter Brook has put it, 'Each moment in Shakespeare should be as important as every other; each speaker should be the "lead" as he speaks.' But the way that Shakespeare is taught is still stuck with the actor-managers of the Victorian stage.

There are three basic ideas which we have taken from the Victorians via Aristotle and which combine to make the study of Shakespeare so tedious:

1. The idea of the Tragic Flaw, which invites us to ask the question 'what is wrong with these people?' and to come up with witheringly useless answers – Macbeth's flaw is ambition, Hamlet's is indecision, Lear's is vanity, Othello's is jealousy. One set of notes widely used in Irish schools, tells us that the Tragic Hero should be 'someone whose misfortunes are brought upon him by some error of judgement on his part. This error of judgement may arise from a flaw in his character, some human weakness. It is essential that to some extent he contributes to his own downfall. A simple "rule of thumb" definition of a Tragic Hero that should be adequate for general purposes might be that he is a potentially noble person who, through some flaw in his character, helps to bring about his own downfall, and who, by suffering, acquires self-knowledge, and so purges his faults.'

The problem with this notion, which is taken directly from Aristotle without any reference to the enormous differences between Greek tragic heroes and Shakespearian ones, is that Shakespeare's plays make no consistent sense when seen in this way. It also means that many of those protagonists can only appear as less than intelligent. If you look at Othello from the point of view that he is merely jealous then it is clear that Othello must not be very intelligent. And if he's not very bright, then he's not very interesting. If Macbeth's ambition is merely a flaw in his character, then he's just another psychopath with an eye for the main chance. If Hamlet's delay is a flaw in his character then he's wasting our time and his own and we are all supposed to believe that killing your uncle is a good thing. If Lear is merely a vain old man, then why does Gloucester have to have his eyes put out? And there is not the slightest evidence that any of Shakespeare's tragic protagonists understand themselves better at the end of the play than at the beginning. They may understand their world better, but that is a very different thing.

The whole idea of the Tragic Flaw presupposes that there is a kind of justice working in Shakespeare's tragedies, that even if the sufferings of the Hero, like those of King Lear, are out of all proportion to his supposed flaw, nevertheless the tragedies are about people bringing destruction on themselves. But this is exactly the opposite of what happens in the plays. The tragedies are littered with innocent corpses, people

9

who have done nothing to bring death on themselves but who nevertheless meet it, often in the most violent and shocking way. Shakespeare goes out of his way in the tragedies to give us meaningless, gratuitous deaths. If jealousy is Othello's flaw, what is Desdemona's? If ambition is Macbeth's flaw, what is Cordelia's? If indecision is Hamlet's flaw, what is Ophelia's? The whole idea of the Tragic Flaw can be maintained only by searching out some evil in Desdemona or Cordelia (as some critics have ludicrously tried to do, ending up with complete nonsense) or by completely separating the heroes from the plays in which we find them, by pretending that Shakespeare wrote his heroes according to one set of rules and everyone else in the plays according to another. Again, Shakespeare comes out looking confused, inconsistent and hardly worth studying.

The real function of the Tragic Flaw theory is to reduce Shakespeare's tragedies, to pretend that they are neat moral fables which we can easily assimilate. It tames the plays and makes them comfortable, bringing them back to a rational little world in which they offer no challenge to our way of looking at things.

2. The idea of the Tragic Hero, which cuts the central character off from the play and then goes on to examine in isolation the characters of all of the other people who affect what happens to him. In Shakespeare, as in all good drama, it is not character that is interesting, but the interplay between characters – the action. If you isolate the individuals in a play and then try to analyse their characters in a static way, they are not only tedious but impossible to understand. C. S. Lewis, who had the experience of marking school exams, put it well, with reference to Chanticleer and Pertelote, a cock and a hen in Chaucer's *Canterbury Tales*: 'I once had a whole batch of School Certificate answers on the *Nun's Priest's Tale* by boys whose form-master was apparently a breeder of poultry. Everything that Chaucer had said in describing Chanticleer and Pertelote was treated by them solely as evidence about the precise breed of these two birds . . . They proved beyond doubt that Chanticleer was very different from our modernised specialised strains and much closer to the old English "barn door fowl". But I couldn't help feeling that they had missed something. I believe that our attention to Hamlet's character in the usual sense misses almost as much.'

The whole idea of looking at character in this sense in Shakespeare's plays is misplaced. Characterization in the modern theatrical sense is a word which only comes into use in the English language in the mid-nineteenth century. Character, in the sense of a part assumed by an actor, comes in a hundred years earlier, but still a very long time after Shakespeare's death. In Shakespeare's time, the word that would have been used in the place of our notion of 'characterization', was 'personation' – the presentation of a person on stage, with obvious overtones of deliberate pretence. To talk about Shakespeare's characters in isolation from the action, to discuss their psychology and motivation, is to treat Shakespearian tragedies as if they were nineteenth-century naturalistic plays. It is to miss their uniqueness and their power. It is also, all too often, to build up a set of stereotypes which take the place of the complex and often deliberately contra-dictory people that Shakespeare gives us.

The idea that there is a set of characters lodged in each Shakespearian play which only needs to be satisfactorily defined in order for us to understand the play, is one which ignores the whole nature of Shakespearian tragedy as theatre. Theatre is historical: the perception of individual theatrical characters changes over time. In the nineteenth century, for instance, Charles Lamb thought it was impossible to actually put *King Lear* on the stage, because 'To see Lear acted is to see an old man tottering about the stage with a walking stick.' Nowadays, no one would dream of a Lear who is either tot-tering or with a walking stick. European poets of the nineteenth century invented a Hamlet who was very like themselves – romantic, enervated, sick at heart. Nowadays we may see Hamlet in our own mould, as a twenty-first century cynic. In the case of Othello, far from agreeing as to the nature of his character, critics and actors have been unable even to agree on the colour of his skin. It may seem per-fectly obvious to us that *Othello* is a story which depends absolutely on the relationship between a black man and a white woman, but to the more openly racist nineteenth cen-tury, even this most obvious aspect of Othello's persona could, indeed must, be overlooked. A. C. Bradley, the Victorian critic from whom many of our ideas about Shakespeare's tragedies come, recognized that Shakespeare had intended Othello to be black, but still thought that this would be more than a modern audience could be expected to stomach: 'Perhaps if we saw Othello coal-black with the bodily eye the aversion of our blood, an aversion which comes as near to being merely physical as anything human can, would overpower our imagination . . .' Because Bradley and his British contemporaries were racist, Othello could not be black, whatever Shakespeare's views on the matter. And Macbeth, whom nineteenth-century critics would have seen as fierce and primitive, could be envisaged in the late twentieth century by an American middle-class writer like Mary McCarthy almost as an American middle-class businessman: 'A commonplace man who talks in commonplaces, a golfer, one might guess.'

What these examples suggest is that it is the way we interpret the play that shapes our understanding of the characters and not the other way round. We decide what it is that the play has to say to us in our own time and then we shape the characters accordingly. And even then we are interested in the characters, not in their character. We want to know how they respond, how they shape and are shaped by all the things and people they encounter. Hamlet's character is only of interest to us if we ever have to write him a job reference. Only if we stick to the idea of the Tragic Flaw, which is a kind of secular version of Original Sin, seeing the people of the plays as ready-assembled packages complete with built-in flaw, does the idea of a fixed character make any sense at all. But the whole point about creations like Lear and Macbeth, Hamlet and Othello is that they have no fixed centre, that they are all response, never quite the same person from one moment to the next, changing even in the course of a single speech perhaps two or three times. At the end of *King Lear* we do not know much more about Lear's character than at the start – what we feel is that we have experienced something extraordinary through him and with him. Shakespeare's tragic protagonists remain enigmatic right to the end. If they didn't we would lose interest in them. They are interesting precisely because they have no fixed characters.

If we try to analyse character in isolation from the dramatic action, what we end up with is scenes which don't make sense. There are many scenes in the tragedies which are about giving us information, in which the people who are speaking are not revealing their characters but telling us what is going on. There are very many others which, as we will see in discussing the individual plays, are impossible to understand if we see them as being about developing the individual characters. And we must also remember that very often the people who talk most about themselves, who give us most material for character analysis, people like Hamlet and Iago, are the very ones who remain enigmatic, whose motives and aims remain most mysterious. We also have to remember that isolating characters from their situation makes for a grossly misleading interpretation of what other characters are like.

One of the reasons why Shakespeare's characters fossilize into stereotypes is that we tend to believe what other characters say about them, without taking into account the dramatic situation, the fact that they may have good reasons to tell lies. Someone like Claudius in *Hamlet*, for instance, gets characterized as a filthy lascivious monster. We don't actually see him being filthy and lascivious, and we know that Hamlet has his own reasons for describing Claudius in this way, but the hunt for a fixed character for Claudius makes it useful to take Hamlet's assessment at face value. What gets overlooked is the fact that the crude language which Hamlet uses when he's talking about Claudius may tell us more about Hamlet than it does about Claudius.

3. The whole idea of the soliloquy, the notion that Shakespeare's heroes spend a great deal of time talking to themselves and, in a kind of spiritual striptease, revealing their true selves to us. It has become fundamental to the teaching of Shakespeare that the soliloquies are the most important part of any tragedy, that they deserve to be isolated, directed and analysed as the real key to the character of the tragic hero. Most guides to Shakespeare will tell you that in soliloquy lies truth. Nothing is more calculated to make Shakespeare's protagonists seem foolish and incomprehensible than the idea that they spend a lot of their days gazing at their navels and talking to themselves. In the plays that Shakespeare wrote, they don't.

Again our idea of the soliloquies is one which comes, not from the seventeenth century but from the nineteenth, in particular from the Romantic movement. The Romantics were interested above all in subjective feeling, in the idea of self-expression. They found, or thought they found, in Shakespeare's soliloquies a subjective form of drama, a kind of theatre that was about self-revelation. The whole centre of interest in Shakespeare's plays came to be located in the soliloquies. Shakespeare's True Confessions were born. And as the nineteenth century went on, the changes that took place in theatrical conventions made the soliloquies look more and more like people talking to themselves. The whole interest in the centrality of the soliloquies as absolutely truthful self-revelation went hand-in-hand with an increasingly psychological notion of character. The soliloquies were important because in them the heroes were revealing their own characters for us.

The problem with all of this is that it has almost nothing to do with the kind of theatre which Shakespeare created and that it blinds us to many of the things that are going on in the plays. It again misses the point that the tragedies are first and foremost plays. In the theatre, it is possible for an actor on stage to speak by himself, but it is not possible for an actor on stage to speak to himself. Unless the actors are really lousy, there is always an audience, always someone listening and watching. The difficulty arises from the fact that since the nineteenth century until the 1960s it was the general convention of theatre that the actors pretend not to notice the audience, and that when they are talking they are talking only to each other. When there is only one actor on the stage, he must be talking to himself. This is a convention which works for a great deal of modern drama.

It has, however, nothing whatsoever to do with Shakespeare. In Shakespeare's theatre there is no convention which says that an actor cannot notice and address the audience. On the contrary, the audience is noticed, winked at, teased and made aware of itself. There is therefore no reason to believe that when an actor is talking alone on stage he is not talking to the audience, that instead of a pure stream of internal monologue the actor is not indirectly addressing the audience. The soliloquies are not, therefore, in any real sense private and internal. They are not, as even a magnificently illuminating critic like Frank Kermode tells us, 'speech in silence, the speech of silence'. They are a form of speech which is somewhere between the private and the public, which tries to marry the concerns of the individual with those of the collective. In the notion of the soliloquies as a pure form of self-expression, it is forgotten that even some of the most intimate soliloquies in *Hamlet* or *Macbeth* use the word 'we' rather than the word 'I'. As a consequence, many of these speeches are almost completely misunderstood.

The way in which this works in individual plays will be discussed in the chapters on those plays, but the important point here is that there is not, in Shakespeare's tragedies, a mere switch between public speech and private speech. There are in fact whole layers of different kinds of speech, ranging from highly formal public exchange to intimate formal conversation, to private informal exchange to different kinds of monologues. By simply focusing on the idea of the soliloquy as the truest form of speech in these plays, you lose the whole drama of the way in which Shakespeare moves all the time from one kind of speech to another, blurring the borders between the private and the public. By not paying attention to the question of who is talking to whom and, more importantly, who is listening in, a great deal of the drama of the plays is lost. First and foremost the soliloquies and all other speeches in Shakespeare are not poems which can be taken out and studied, they are pieces of dramatic action.

3. So What is Tragedy?

Shakespeare, as we have seen, chose to ignore the Aristotelian rules for tragedy, and it is therefore absurd to analyse Shakespeare's tragedies as if they were versions of the Greek model. It's not that Shakespeare didn't know the rules. He positively decided that a different kind of theatre was needed if he was to successfully dramatize his own society. The most famous work of literary criticism of Elizabethan England was Sir Philip Sidney's *Defence of Poesie*. In it Sidney laid down the Aristotelian rules: 'The stage should always represent but one place, and the uttermost time presupposed in it should be, both by Aristotle's precept and common reason, but one day. Moreover tragedy and comedy must be kept severely apart and the playwright should not thrust in the clown by head and shoulders to play a part in majestical matters.' Shakespeare, of course, broke all of these rules and knew he was breaking them. He presents a kaleidoscope of places and a broad sweep of time. His clowns are always thrusting their way into majestical matters. He didn't break the rules, though, because he wasn't up to writing classical plays on the Greek and Roman lines. He could do it if he wanted to: *The Comedy of Errors* uses a single place and a single day. *Julius Caesar* is a perfect classical tragedy. He broke them because they were not good enough to deal with the complexities of the world he was living in. *Hamlet, Macbeth, King Lear,* and *Othello* are tragedies but tragedies of a kind which cannot be analysed in terms of tragic flaws and tragic heroes. To understand what kind of tragedies they are, we have to understand what kind of world they were intended to reflect.

Successful tragedy is not particularly common in the long history of the theatre. It gets written only at certain times, times when there is an overwhelming tension between two sets of values, two world views, two ways of thinking about how individuals relate to their societies. The tragic figures are those who get caught in the middle between these two world views, and who therefore literally can do nothing right. They can do nothing right because what is right in one world is not right in another. They act according to one set of values in a world that is still dominated by a different set of values. Clear distinctions, the borders between things that are supposed to be opposite, are breaking down. The interesting and dramatic thing about people in a tragedy is that they are caught on those borders.

What was England like in Shakespeare's time? For one thing it was highly stratified and the division between rich and poor was overwhelmingly obvious. On the one hand, between a third and a half of the population lived at subsistence level and was chronically under-employed. On the other hand, at the top, there was the traditional landed elite, now challenged for power by the rising professional groups: merchants, lawyers, clergymen and administrative officials. The landowners and professional classes, though only five per cent of the popula- tion, between them enjoyed a larger proportion of the national income than did all the lower classes (over fifty per cent of the population) put together.

The social elite of Shakespeare's time was highly educated, and shortly after Shakespeare's death it was estimated that about two and a half per cent of the young male population was receiving some form of third level education, a proportion that would not be attained again in England until well into the twentieth century. But at the same time between half and two thirds of the adult population was unable to read. There was no simple, unified, primitive world, therefore, but a highly divided and diverse society, where social and intellectual change had long been at work, moving in many different directions. It was a world of religious, geographical and economic novelties, where, at the same time, the pull of the old order was still powerful. This sense of large, incompatible forces rubbing up against each other has been captured by the great Shakespeare director Grigori Kozintsev: 'Everything was shuffled – the groan of death with the cry of birth. The lash whistled in medieval torture chambers, but the click of abacus balls was heard all the louder. Feudal outlaws discussed the price of wool, and rumours about the success of Flemish textiles were intermingled with authentic details of the witches' Sabbath.'

So what should be the most obvious thing about Shakespeare's time is that it is a period of rapid change, of the transition between one world view and another. This obvious fact was obscured by the nineteenth-century critics who wanted to look back on Elizabethan England as a Golden Age, a time of order, stability and a fixed universe, and to view Shakespeare in this light. This is where the notion of Shakespeare as timeless, as the bearer of universal values, comes from. But in fact Shakespeare's time is anything but stable, and his tragedies are plays which dramatize traumatic change and the way it affects our whole way of looking at the world.

It was certainly obvious to Shakespeare's contemporaries that they were living through a period of crisis. Five years before Shakespeare's death, the poet John Donne wrote that:

> 'Tis all in pieces, all coherence gone;
> All just supply and all relation:
> Prince, subject, father, son, are things forgot,
> For every man alone thinks he hath got
> To be a Phoenix and that then can be
> None of that kind of which he is but he.
> This is the world's condition now . . .

('The First Anniversary', 1611)

Looking at his and Shakespeare's England, Donne saw a world in which all order and coherence had fallen apart, in which the hierarchy of relations both within the state and within the family was breaking down, in which men were getting the idea that they were uniquely their own invention rather than the product of their place and status within a highly stratified society. His poem could also have been an exact description of Shakespeare's tragedies, of the inter-related breakdown of family and state in each of them, of the phoenix-like Lear and Hamlet and Macbeth and Othello, each believing that he is a self-made man, that he owes his individuality not to his status but to his free will. Their tragedy is that their world is not yet quite like that, that the pull of order and hierarchy is still very strong, not least within their own minds. The tragedies are about the conflict between status on the one hand and individual power on the other, and what dooms Othello, Lear, Macbeth and Hamlet is that for none of them do status and power go together at the same time.

Shakespeare's age is one in which a whole new class, the capitalist and professional middle class, comes to substantial power and prominence in England. Elizabethan England depended on foreign trade and foreign trade led to the rise of merchant capital. The making of large amounts of money by a new class of people who were neither the traditional land-owning elite nor the mass of peasants and labourers meant that Shakespeare's lifetime became the period of the most rapid advance in mining and manufacture that England was to know until the Industrial Revolution of the late eighteenth century. And at the same time, the centralisation of state power and the beginnings of a foreign trading empire made necessary the development of a large professional, educated, administrative class. These people in turn brought the new humanist Renaissance ideas into vogue in England. Both economically and intellectually, therefore, the fixed hierarchy of the old feudal order was being challenged as never before. There are two value systems, two world views in competition, and this is the essential context in which to understand Shakespeare's tragedies.

The extent of the changes which were underway in Shakespeare's times cannot be overstated. James I, who was on the throne when all of the major tragedies except *Hamlet* were written, preached that kings ruled by Divine Right and many political writers argued that the property of every subject should be completely at the disposal of the king. Within thirty-five years of Shakespeare's death, the English had executed their king and politics was being conducted as a rational inquiry, a matter of utility, experience and common sense. James I wrote a treatise on witches, and was no more superstitious than most of his educated middle-class subjects, who nevertheless took alchemy and astrology very seriously indeed. By the second half of the seventeenth century, science was in the ascendant and fairies, witches and astrology were no longer respectable beliefs for an educated man to hold. In Shakespeare's time, the earth was the centre of a universe in which God and the Devil continuously intervened. In the second half of the century in which the tragedies were written, Newton would show the universe to be a self-moving machine. A world in which everything, both natural and supernatural, had its proper place and category, was giving way to one in which both society and the universe seemed to be made up of competing atoms. Shakespeare's tragedies were written at a time when nothing less than a fundamental reordering of our understanding of the world, the categories by which we make sense of our experience, was in progress. The plays contain and dramatize that reordering and to fail to understand this is to fail to understand the plays.

Shakespeare can properly be described as part of the English Renaissance but only if the Renaissance is understood in certain ways. We think of the Renaissance as the time in which European culture repossessed the cultural artefacts of the classical Greek and Roman civilization, and because Shakespeare is a Renaissance figure this encourages the tendency to think of him in terms of that classical world, in particular of Aristotle and Greek tragedy. But this is to misunderstand both Shakespeare and the Renaissance. The repossession of Greek and Roman antiquity is not so much a statement of continuity, of the continuance of classical into modern Europe. It is the opposite, for to repossess something implies a recognition of precisely how different it is from your own culture. The success of the Renaissance presupposed the recognition of a fundamental discontinuity between the culture of the present and that of the distant past. It implies that you have started to think of your own culture, not as absolute, which was the feudal conception of the Middle Ages, but as relative, as something to which there are fundamentally different alternatives. Shakespeare is a Renaissance writer only in the sense that he is aware of the extent to which nothing is absolute. In the tragedies there is an overwhelming feeling that all of the most fundamental values of society have become relative.

This raises another of the hoary clichés about Shakespeare that most of us acquire in our schooldays. It is an article of faith, again taken from Aristotle, that in Shakespearian tragedy the downfall of the hero must seem inevitable. One set of study notes on *King Lear*, for instance, tell us at the outset that 'In tragedy, the hero's fall is inevitable, and presented as being so. The tragic dramatist organises his world in such a way that the chances of a happy outcome are nil.' This is largely true of Greek drama where in general a train of action has been set in motion long before the play even opens and cannot be undone. There is a cold logic working itself out and we can but sit and watch as it reaches towards its inevitable conclusion. But this is almost completely untrue of Shakespeare. In Shakespeare there is no cold logic and indeed no logic at all. It is not inevitable that Othello should kill Desdemona, indeed it is amazing that he should do so. It is not inevitable that Cordelia should be hanged, indeed the whole point of it is that it is utterly gratuitous. It is not inevitable that Hamlet should die, indeed Shakespeare goes out of his way to make his death messy, complicated, fumbled. Far from it being inevitable that Macbeth should be killed, Shakespeare goes to great lengths to make his death a refutation of the idea of inevitability, since the prophecies which imply that everything is preordained, turn out to be no more than verbal tricks.

The doctrine of inevitability implies an absolute world, a world in which once the stone is dropped in the pool, the ripples will be unstoppable. Shakespeare on the other hand gives us a relative world, a world in which causes don't have their effects, in which almost nothing is predictable, never mind inevitable. A stone is dropped in one pool and the ripples spread in another, seemingly miles away. Shakespeare is not concerned with a logical universe but with an irrational one, made irrational by the fact that it contains two different sets of values, two separate logics, which refuse to hold their places.

In all four of the major tragedies, the central figure is some-one who loses a sense of himself, whose grip on his own identity becomes weaker and weaker, leading to real or feigned madness (in the case of Hamlet and Lear) or to the kind of complete dependence on the words and judgements of others which is the mark of a loss of faith in one's own independent identity (Macbeth with the witches, Othello with Iago). This reflects the fact that in Shakespeare's time there is a transition in the whole way in which one's identity is defined. In feudal, medieval society, your identity is your role, and your role is determined by your birth and position, so long as that birth is legitimate. Legitimate birth confers not just a right of inheritance but a whole set of duties and prescribed behaviour. If you want to know who you are, you examine your position in society. You are your status. In the kind of commercial, capitalist world which is emerging in Shakespeare's time, you are your power. Your identity is the sum of your achievements. It is something you make for yourself. You are what you do. The tragedy of Lear and Macbeth, of Hamlet and Othello, is that they think they operate according to both of these principles, that they can base themselves both on a world of status and a world of power, even though these two worlds are contradictory and in active conflict.

It is the fate of these four men to enjoy either status or power, but never both together. Hamlet, as a royal prince who has been denied succession to the throne, has status but not power. Othello, as a mercenary general admired for his skill but disdained for his colour, has power but no status. Lear, keeping the title of king but not the reality of the office, has status but no power. Macbeth, killing Duncan, gains power but not status; not that most essential aspect of what it means to hold a hereditary office, the right to hand on his kingship to his children and his children's children in an unbroken assertion of order and tradition. Power and status are two worlds, two governing values, one from the new capitalist world, the other from the old feudal one, which refuse to come together for any of the great tragic figures of Shakespeare's plays. And it is in the failure of this equation, the fact that they are caught between two worlds, that they are lost.

Shakespeare, of course, doesn't present us with abstractions called 'power' and 'status' in his plays; he gives us people trying to live their lives. And the way in which this conflict is played out is in the relationship between men and women. In each of the four plays, a man becomes separated from a woman. Lear loses Cordelia, Hamlet loses Ophelia, Othello loses Desdemona, Macbeth loses Lady Macbeth. And in each the woman who is lost represents the man's link to an ordered, traditional society. For Lear, it is Cordelia who puts forward the notion of proper degree and proportion in things, of everything having its proper place. Losing her, he loses his connection to that ordered, feudal world. For Hamlet, it is Ophelia who might represent marriage, loyalty, traditional morality. For Othello, adrift in the wild world of war, it is Desdemona who represents due fidelity, respectable society, the established moral order. For Macbeth, it is Lady Macbeth, haunted by the demands of conscience, duty and the proper order of things, who comes to represent the moral universe with which he has broken. With the women representing one set of values and the men another, it is hardly surprising that men and women cannot function together in any kind of wholeness in these plays, that the sexual order as well the social and political order, breaks down.

This is why images of childlessness, of sterility, of the lack of continuity between the generations, are such powerful images in these tragedies. If men and women cannot fit together in

27

harmony, then sterility looms. Hamlet condemns Ophelia to sterility. ('Get thee to a nunnery.') The extent of Lady Macbeth's unnaturalness is measured by her rhetorical willingness to murder the baby at her breast. The farthest reach of her husband's madness is not the murder of his king or of his friend but that of Macduff's little children. When Macduff hears of the event his curse on Macbeth (leading to all sorts of contortions on the part of literal-minded commentators as to whether the Macbeths have children or not) is 'He has no children.' When Macbeth himself wants to express the ultimate horror he can imagine, it is the killing of the seeds of future generations: 'though the treasure of all nature's germens tumble together / Even till destruction sicken.' And the very same image appears at the climax of *King Lear*. 'Crack nature's molds, all germens spill at once.' In Shakespeare's tragedies, things are changing so fast that the whole idea of human continuity seems to be threatened. There is even, in *King Lear*, a powerful sense that the end of the world may be at hand.

It is not, though, just the content and the imagery of Shakespeare's tragedies that is shaped by the extremely fluid nature of the world he lives in, it is also the kind of poetry he writes. Shakespeare's iambic pentameter is not just a matter of individual style. It is a form of poetic rhythm that is superbly well adapted to include a whole range of contradictory things. It is free and boundless, able to sweep over an extraordinary range of dramatic situations (from the very intimate to the formal and public) and a huge diversity of speaking characters. But at the same time it also retains a strong sense of order, of shape and of form. The whole nature of the poetry embodies the contradictions that Shakespeare is dramatizing: the oppostition between order on the one hand and individuality on the other, between feudalism and capitalism. And it is precisely the containing power of this poetry, the extraordinary inclusiveness of it, that gives the tragedies their formal rigour, the feeling that in spite of the fierce tensions they contain, they are still finished, ordered works of art. The plays invoke chaos without themselves being chaotic.

4. Toads, Toenails and Puritans

The momentous social changes that were taking place in Shakespeare's time help us to understand the kind of conflicts that are going on in his plays. But they don't really tell us all that much about the way the plays work, about how they affect us, about what it is that we feel in watching the plays and why. To understand that we have to ask how the conflicts of Shakespeare's time could be expressed in ways that would seem to have a powerful gut effect on us. And to do that we have to understand something about the nature of tragedy as a social ritual.

All societies, whether they are what we would regard as primitive, tribal societies, or as modern sophisticated ones, have their rituals, and in general these rituals have similar functions. The main function of public rituals is to help us to put an order on our experience, to give us categories through which we can make sense of the multiplicity of the world in which we live. Rituals are basically systems of classification, the

simplest ones being organized around the most basic oppositions: left and right, black and white, male and female. They
classify things as either one thing or the other, making us comfortable with our experience. And in all societies which have
rituals, therefore, things which defy categorization, which slip
between opposites, which refuse to be one thing or the other,
are dangerous and powerful. Shakespeare's tragic protagonists
are just such things, and his tragedies are rituals in which those
dangerous and powerful things are contained. Shakespeare's
tragedies come from a culture in which the whole idea of ritual
is very much a public question. He writes at the time of the
Protestant Reformation, a reformation which presents itself as
a deliberate attempt to take the ritual out of religion, to destroy
the idea that public religious ceremonies have any ritual or
magical function. Significantly, the most radical of the
Protestants, the Puritans, saw theatre in the same category as
superstitions and rituals, wanting to take the theatricality out of
religion and then, after Shakespeare's death, to ban theatre
altogether, a step that was absolutely in line with their attitude
to religious ceremony.

It's important to realize that for the people of Shakespeare's
time and before, religion was not so much a set of beliefs as a
set of rituals, and that therefore the loss of those rituals with
the rise of Protestantism left a large gap to be filled. As the historian Keith Thomas has put it 'The church was important . . .
not because of its formalised code of belief but because its rites
were an essential accompaniment to the important events
in . . . life – birth, marriage, death . . . Religion was a ritual
method of living, not a set of dogmas.' With the changeover to

Protestantism, the religious rituals were abandoned or reduced, but the anxieties which created the need for them had not disappeared: 'the fluctuations of nature, the hazards of fire, the threat of plague and disease, the fear of evil spirits, and all the uncertainties of daily life'. And indeed to all of these uncertainties was added the uncertainty of unprecedented economic, political and cultural change. There were needs and no rituals to fill them. The theatre, and in particular Shakespeare, was one way of providing for that need.

In creating his tragedies as secular rituals, Shakespeare shows all categories, all basic opposites, breaking down. In the tragedies, the basic opposites by which we are able to make sense of things – life and death, black and white, man and woman – melt into each other. Shakespeare is dealing with a world that is reordering its knowledge, with the rise of a class whose first triumphant assault on power 150 years later will be, not the storming of the Bastille, but the writing, by Diderot and D'Alembert, of an *Encyclopaedia*, a new classification of everything that is known. But in Shakespeare's time, that new classification has not yet emerged. The *Summa Theologica* of Saint Thomas Aquinas, which classified all knowledge for the medieval world, is no longer good enough, and the *Encyclopaedia* of Diderot and D'Alembert has not yet been written. Since there is no satisfactory way of categorizing experience, things refuse to hold their identity and begin to slip into each other, becoming both powerful and dangerous. It is just such things that rituals are there to deal with and it is just such things which make up Shakespeare's tragedies.

Things and people which refuse to stay within their proper boundaries both fascinate and horrify us. As a consequence they take on ritual significance. Monsters like the elephant man and the wolf boy are fascinating because they defy the boundaries of the categories which we use to order our experience. Certain animals make our skin crawl because they slip between categories: slimy reptiles that refuse to belong to either the sea or the land; nasty rodents that come into our houses yet refuse to conform to the bounds of domestication. In-between animals, those that are neither fish nor flesh, take on special meaning and ritual value. Similarly, toenails or hair, those things which are on the border between ourselves and the material world outside us, go into magic potions. The animals in the witches' brew in *Macbeth* – toads, cats, hedge pigs, snakes, newts, frogs, bats, lizards – are all ambiguous as either reptiles or half-domestic, half-wild. It is not for nothing that the witches chant 'Double, double': all of these things have double meanings and are therefore dangerous. Throughout the tragedies, as we shall see in looking at the individual plays, the imagery is of snakes, monsters, humans turning into animals and animals turning into humans, creatures that exist on the dangerous borders between categories. The plays themselves are a kind of witches' brew, where dangerous visions are conjured up in a powerful ritual.

For what is true of animals is even more true of people. Rituals everywhere are very concerned with people who go beyond the normal boundaries, who escape from their proper categories. Tribes have rituals in which a man will leave his band and wander in the forest in the guise of a madman, rituals based on the belief that by leaving the order of society and going out into chaos and disorder some kind of power can be gained. These rituals journey into disorder in a double sense – venturing both beyond the confines of society and into the disordered regions of the mind. Most obviously, this is what happens to King Lear, but in all of the tragedies (though in *Othello* less than the others, for reasons which will be discussed in the chapter on that play) there are marginal figures, people who are neither one thing nor the other – ghosts, witches, Banquo's unborn heirs, the dead Yorick in *Hamlet* who is momentarily brought back to life, Poor Tom in the heath scene in *King Lear*.

The protagonists of Shakespeare's tragedies themselves conform to what the anthropologist Mary Douglas has to say about figures who take on ritual significance in tribal societies, who are both dangerous and fascinating: 'Danger lies in transitional states, simply because transition is neither one state nor the next, it is indefinable.' Living in a time of transition, Shakespeare gives us tragic protagonists who are dangerous and powerful, who slip between all of the categories of our experience, and who therefore have about them the fundamental power of ritual. It is not because we can define their characters that Shakespeare's people are interesting to us, but because they are literally indefinable, eluding and denying definition in a deliberate and systematic way. It is not because they teach us lessons that we care about them, but because they enact something that is dangerous, powerful and disturbing.

2

Hamlet: Dying as an Art

1. The Making of a Slob

Hamlet is a slob, a shirker. He has a job to do and won't do it. He keeps persuading himself that there is a good reason for not getting on with the job in hand. He is certainly unwell and possibly evil. The problem of *Hamlet* is Hamlet. Hamlet is there to teach us a lesson: when faced with a difficult and unpalatable task, we must stiffen out upper lips, put our consciences in the deep freeze, and get on with it. Otherwise, we will come to a bad end.

Alternatively: yes, Hamlet is guilty of delay and indecision, but this is a flaw in an essentially noble nature. He is a melancholy intellectual in black tights, leaning up against a headstone with a skull in his hand. The play happens not in the castle at Elsinore but in the soul of Hamlet. It is a beautiful soul, far too beautiful to be befouled with something as vulgar as action. 'A beautiful, pure, noble and most moral nature, without the strength of nerve which makes the hero, sinks beneath a burden which it can neither bear nor throw off', writes Goethe. Hamlet is a 'pale cavalier', writes Arthur Rimbaud. Hamlet is gorgeous, dressed in a feathered hat and velvet clothes. He wraps his hand in a silk handkerchief before he picks up the skull in the graveyard. His fashion accessories, like his soul, are the height of melancholy chic. The nineteenth-century French painter Eugène Delacroix publishes a series of illustrations of Hamlet – young, delicate, beautifully pensive, his face devoid of passion, sarcasm, vulgarity. Critics start to judge the performances of actors playing Hamlet, not in relation to how well they make sense of Shakespeare's play, but by how well they match Delacroix's illustrations.

These two versions of Hamlet are two sides of the one coin, and in both Hamlet becomes uninteresting: either a slob or a poseur. Neither, as it happens, has very much to do with Shakespeare's play. Both have everything to do with the preconception that *Hamlet* is a tragedy of the Aristotelian sort, a play about a tragic hero with a fatal flaw and an inevitable doom. Hamlet poses great problems for the tragic hero theory because he is patently not a hero. He doesn't do what the tragic hero is supposed to do – descend from the top of fortune's wheel to the bottom. He is, rather, at a low ebb when we first see him and remains on the same plane throughout the play. Far from being a play driven by the logic of inevitability, meanwhile, *Hamlet* is extraordinarily illogical, with its plays-within-plays, sea journeys, graveyards, pirates, drowning, madness. Far from the ending having the neat feeling of fated retribution, it is a wildly messy heap of bodies, sordid and nasty, the result of 'purposes mistook'. If *Hamlet* was to be rescued for the irrelevant Aristotelian definition of tragedy, only one thing remained – the tragic flaw. More than any of the other tragedies, *Hamlet* has been explained in terms of the tragic flaw, and more than any of the others it has been obscured.

The idea that the character of Hamlet is the only thing really worth looking at in the play and that his character, whether noble or evil, is essentially flawed, has been an extraordinarily persistent feature of the way the play has been written about, directed and taught. It is the main line of *Hamlet* criticism, running from Richardson, Goethe, Coleridge, Schlegel and Hazlitt through the Romantics and into the psychological and psychoanalytic obsessions of the twentieth century. The question is Hamlet's delay in doing what he ought to do and the answer must lie in Hamlet's tantalizingly mysterious psyche. The last thing that needs to be done is to look at *Hamlet* as a play and as a play by Shakespeare.

The constant theme is the idea that Hamlet is the problem, that he has a disease which we must diagnose. G. Wilson Knight, for instance, tells us that 'To Hamlet comes the command of a great act – revenge . . . a sick soul is commanded to heal, to cleanse, to create harmony. But good cannot come of evil: it is seen that the sickness of his soul only further infects the state – his disintegration spreads out, disintegrating.' Derek Traversi talks about 'the disease, which emanating from Hamlet himself, expands from his wounded nature to cover the

36

entire action'. The doctrine of Original Sin, of which the notion of the tragic flaw is a secular version, is given a whole new life in Freudian psychoanalysis. Ernest Jones's very influential study of Hamlet from a Freudian point of view sees him a sick patient on the consulting couch: 'Throughout the play we have the clearest picture of a man who sees his duty plain before him, but who shirks it at every opportunity and suffers in consequence the most intense remorse.'

What we end up with in this tradition of analysis is a clinical report on Hamlet that has almost nothing to do with the play: 'Hamlet had, in years gone by, as a child, bitterly resented having to share his mother's affection, even with his own father, had regarded him as a rival and had secretly wished him out of the way so that he might enjoy undisputed and undisturbed the monopoly of that affection . . . Without his being in the least aware of it, these ancient desires are ringing in his mind, are once more struggling to find conscious expression and need such an expenditure of energy again to repress them that he is reduced to the deplorable mental state he himself so vividly depicts.' Thus, there are no soldiers, no political power struggles, no invading armies, no competing ideas about life and death and eventually not even a king who has killed Hamlet's father and usurped his throne. Claudius is nothing other than Hamlet himself: 'He of course detests [Claudius] but it is the jealous detestation of one evil-doer towards his successful fellow . . . In reality his uncle incorporates the deepest and most buried part of his own personality, so that he cannot kill him without also killing himself. This solution is actually the one that Hamlet finally adopts.'

All of this is absurd, because it ignores the whole context and action of the play, but it merely takes to a logical conclusion a long history of interpretation in which the real play takes place in Hamlet's mind and everything else is either irrelevant or a projection of Hamlet's psyche. The view of Hamlet as at worst evil and at best mentally ill and defective in nerve and guts did not die with the Victorians but was renewed in the modern theatre. The American director Charles Marowitz writes that 'I despise Hamlet. He is a slob, a talker, an analyser, a rationaliser. Like the parlour liberal or the paralysed intellectual, he can describe every facet of a problem, yet never pull his finger out. Is Hamlet a coward, as he himself suggests, or simply a poseur, a frustrated actor who plays the scholar, the courtier and the soldier as an actor (a very bad actor) assumes a variety of different roles? And why does he keep saying everything twice? And how can someone talk so pretty in such a rotten country with the sort of work he's got cut out for him? You may think he's a sensitive well-spoken fellow but, frankly, he gives me a pain in the ass.'

Or, less bluntly, the English director Jonathan Miller puts it like this: 'I have always been interested in the idea of Hamlet as a rather unattractive character, a tiresome, clever, destructive boy who is very intelligent but volatile, dirty-minded and immature. This interpretation does not subvert the intelligence of the speeches even though we are usually given the noble Dane as a philosophical and restrained character whose reluctance to revenge is prompted by a fastidious refusal to indulge in bloody and inelegant actions. It may well be that he is also a childish creature full of tantrums and resentments who, in a purely Freudian way, is reluctant to kill the object that he seems to hate because, by keeping Claudius, the object of his hatred, alive he can ignore the person he might have loathed even more – his father . . . Hamlet can then indulge in self-deluding fantasies of affection for his dead father.'

Both Marowitz and Miller are right. Seen in the way they want us to see him, Hamlet is a pain in the ass and a tiresome boy. Were it not for the fortunate fact that Shakespeare wrote a different play, Hamlet would not be worth our attention. In Shakespeare's play, Hamlet's delay is simply not the issue. Apart from the soliloquies, in which Hamlet sometimes struggles with himself about the duties he has and the options open to him, there are only two occasions in the play when Hamlet's failure or refusal to act is underlined. The first is the single occasion when he actually spurns the opportunity to kill Claudius. The second is when the ghost endorses his suggestion that he is 'tardy'. In both cases, however, it is Hamlet's conception of his role, of what he must do and how he must do it, that is in question, not the mere idea of delay.

Shakespeare, moreover, deliberately gives us two alternative role models for Hamlet, both of whom fit the mould of the all-action hero the critics want him to be. He has Hamlet contemplate Young Fortinbras and his headlong rush to war and possible death. Fortinbras is a man of action who does not scruple about moral consequences. But we have also just heard that Fortinbras's quest is abject folly – 'a little patch of ground', a 'straw' (4, 4). Hamlet, in seeming to admire Fortinbras, takes up this word 'straw', this image of futility – 'to find quarrel in a straw when honour's at stake'. How could such a man as

Fortinbras offer an acceptable model of action for Hamlet, who is so sceptical about the worth of all this blind courage and inflated ambition? And the other possible model, Laertes, who does what Hamlet will not do – drop all hesitancy and all scruple about the afterlife – is, at the time he does so, a pawn, a tool of Claudius who, while he thinks he is exercising free will, is in fact being manipulated by a consummate politician. There is no model of action for Hamlet. What Shakespeare gives us is not a slob or a shirker or a mother-fixated neurotic, but a man of action – the man to whom everyone turns at the start of the play when there is a crisis, the man who can board a pirate ship, the man who has few scruples about killing those he sees as threatening him. He is concerned with how, not whether, to perform his task. He is concerned with perfecting his role on a very tricky and untrustworthy stage.

2. The Corrupted Currents

There is not a single character in *Hamlet*, with the possible exception of Young Fortinbras, who sees the political and social world in which the action unfolds as anything other than corrupt, rotten, nasty and sordid. And Young Fortinbras is both a fool and a liar, a man who is willing to sacrifice his own and other people's lives for the sake of a worthless piece of ground, and to break a solemn political undertaking when he sees an opportunity for power and advantage in doing so. *Hamlet* is unusual among Shakespeare's plays in that it has no stated ideal of good government, no great vision of the social order which has been disrupted. Things have gone too far for people, even the very top people, to fool themselves. The king, Claudius, knows all about backhanders and bending the rules:

> In the corrupted currents of this world
> Offence's gilded hand may shove by justice,
> And oft 'tis seen the wicked prize itself
> Buys out the law. (3, 3, 57–)

The Prince, Hamlet, looks around him and sees little except injustice and tyranny:

> Th' oppressor's wrong, the proud man's contumely,
> The pangs of disprized love, the law's delay,
> The insolence of office, and the spurns
> That patient merit of th'unworthy takes . . . (3, 1, 73–)

The Lord Chamberlain, Polonius, when he wants to advise his son how to protect himself in the world, takes it for granted that that world is a dangerous and untrustworthy place: be slow to make friends, don't let yourself be in anybody's debt, keep your ears open and, whatever you say, say nothing. (1, 3, 59–) The Lord Chamberlain's son, when he wants to advise his sister, takes it for granted that men are dangerous and untrustworthy: don't listen to fine words, don't be taken in, don't even show yourself to the moon or you'll be ruined, live in constant fear: 'Fear it, Ophelia, fear it, my dear sister . . .' (1, 3, 30–)

The first thing we see in *Hamlet* is the jumpiness of the soldiers on the battlements. These are the king's guards, in the
royal castle, the centre of power and administration in
Denmark. And yet they are jittery, cautious, watchful. The first
words we hear are the fretful 'Who's there?' This is a place in
which anyone might sneak up on you, a play in which you
have to be on your guard. Lovers in their intimate moments
are watched from behind walls, a man saying his prayers is
spied on. Everything may be overheard. People hide behind
curtains and pillars. Bedrooms and the palace itself can be
invaded by an angry son, an angry mob, a conquering army.
'The architecture of Elsinore,' says Grigory Kozintsev, 'does
not consist of walls but of the ears the walls have. There are
doors, the better to eavesdrop behind, windows the better to
spy from. The walls are made up of guards. Every sound gives
birth to echoes, repercussions, whispers, rustling.' In *Macbeth*,
when a ghost comes to visit Macbeth, no one else can see him.
The drama of the scene is that it is a private moment in a
public situation. In *Hamlet*, when a ghost comes to see the
Prince, everyone else sees, indeed everyone else seems to know
about it before Hamlet does. In *Hamlet*, no one is ever really
surprised by anything that happens. It merely confirms what
they already suspect. Even when a dead man's bones are found
in a grave, everything is already known about who he is, what
he was like, what he did for a living. Even when a ghost reveals
the terrible secret he has come all the way from the other side of
death to deliver, it turns out to be no more than a confirmation
of what is already guessed at. When Hamlet hears that
Claudius killed his father, his words are 'O my prophetic soul.'

In the world of *Hamlet*, when the King of Denmark sends a secret letter to the King of England, it is opened, tampered with, its contents altered. Nothing is secret, nothing private. *Hamlet*, indeed, is about the most public play it is possible to imagine. That it has become the very type of the private play, a play that takes place within a man's silent thoughts, is a mark of the distortions that have befallen it over time.

Hamlet has come to be thought of as a play of soliloquies, thus a play dominated by a man talking to himself. In fact, *Hamlet* is in no way exceptional for the amount of monologue it has. Eight per cent of it is monologue. There is almost twice as much monologue in *Macbeth*, a play generally thought of as full of incident and action. Hamlet's own soliloquies are six per cent of the play, and only half of these involve him using the word 'I'. Many of the soliloquies, including those like the 'To be or not to be' speech which are regarded as the most isolated and internal, use the word 'we' and are opened out on to a vision of the society in which Hamlet lives, placing him among, not apart from, his fellow men.

The world of *Hamlet* is Shakespeare's own. Looking at it without all the accumulated preconceptions, we remember that it is written by a man living in the first efficient police state, a writer whose two most important predecessors have recently met their deaths at the hands of the secret police: Christopher Marlowe, murdered as part of a dark political plot; Thomas Kyd, whose *Spanish Tragedy* is one of the direct inspirations of *Hamlet*, mortally broken by torture. It is Shakespeare's own, too, in that it is a place where long-established divisions of rank and class are coming under pressure. In that world, and not just in the court, trust and order have broken down. Claudius calls the ordinary people 'the distracted multitude' and tells Laertes that he has reason to fear them, that he can't get rid of Hamlet because the people love him. Claudius talks of 'the people muddied, / Thick and unwholesome in their thoughts and whispers.' (4, 5, 79–80) Their thoughts and whispers are monitored too: the King knows what lies in the dark spaces of their minds, what they mutter quietly in the streets. Their insolence is that of a changing world, in which feudal distinctions of class and rank are threatened. Hamlet remarks to Horatio that social distinctions are breaking down, that it is getting hard to tell the difference between a peasant and a lord: 'By the Lord, Horatio, these three years I have taken note of it. The age is grown so picked that the toe of the peasant comes so near the heel of the courtier that he galls his kibe.' (5, 1, 134–) And as the play goes on, the ordinary people become more and more threatening, more and more an insistent player in the drama. They want a new world, a world in which the accepted hierarchy will be forgotten. They follow Laertes to the very door of Claudius's office with their clamouring:

> The rabble call him lord;
> And as the world were but now to begin,
> Antiquity forgot, custom unknown,
> The ratifiers and props of every word,
> They cry 'Choose we: Laertes shall be king'. (4, 5, 98–)

The old order has sunk into corruption, tyranny and decay. The individual is crowded out by the overweening vigilance of a dying state and the surging rage of the multitude. The new order is frightening – the mob howling at the door, all customs thrown out, all promises broken. The Gentleman who reports on the rabble imagines it to be like a terrifying sea sweeping over the land, a fierce and elemental force blotting out all features, all individuality. And, most significantly, he describes it as a breaking of boundaries: 'overpeering of his list'. The breaking of boundaries is dangerous. It is what threatens identity, individuality. Hamlet's tragedy is that he is caught between this old order and this new one, sharing some of the values of both, desperately trying to keep his individuality alive.

3. The Dead

Hamlet is a play about death. Or rather, it is a play about the survival of the individual in the face of death. But this is neither merely a metaphysical or mystical problem, nor a matter of Hamlet's morbid psychology. It is not about a man in black tights looking into the empty eye sockets of a skull. It is a real question, rooted in the life of Shakespeare's time. He and his contemporaries would have lived with death that was everyday and everywhere. There had always been death, of course, death in great numbers and death at an early age. What was different about Shakespeare's time was the sense that this might not be the normal and natural state of affairs, but that death was a real loss. What you have in Shakespeare's time is, on the one hand, an educated elite, and on the other, a condition of life for the overwhelming majority of people that is characterized by pain, sickness and premature death. Even among the nobility, whose chances of living a long life were much better than those of the poor, the life expectation at birth of boys was less than thirty. Today it would be well over seventy. 'We shall find more who have died within thirty or thirty-five years of age than passed it,' wrote a contemporary of Shakespeare's. Even those who died could expect a great deal of physical pain, since very many people suffered from one chronic illness or another, at least in part because of a poor diet. Epidemics were common and disastrous – when Shakespeare had to leave London in 1593, 15,000 people died of plague. Ten years later, the death toll was 30,000, or over a sixth of the city's population. Poverty, sickness and sudden disaster were the most familiar features of the social environment. The difference now was that you had, for the first time, a reasonably large educated elite that was beginning to think that these things might not have to be the norm of life. In this lies the seeds of a tragic vision, the vision that is at the heart of *Hamlet*.

Hamlet himself, we know, is a humanist. He is a member of the new educated elite, has been to Wittenberg University, is full of the new philosophy of his time. He sees every man as a potential god, is almost convinced of the Renaissance glorification of his species. But he is also inescapably aware of death, of its power to reduce all of this to nothing. 'What a piece of work is a man,' he says, 'How noble in reason, how infinite in faculty; in form and moving, how express and admirable, in action how like an angel, in apprehension how like a god – the beauty of the world, the paragon of animals!'

46

But then, remembering death, he immediately adds 'And yet to me what is this quintessence of dust?' (2, 2, 304–) Hamlet cannot think of life without thinking of death, of death without thinking of life. (It is a mark of the distortion of Shakespeare's play, the obsession with Hamlet's psychology as opposed to what he actually thinks, that in the most widely seen version of the play in the last fifty years, Laurence Olivier's film, this whole speech about man is simply cut out.) What is dangerous and powerful about *Hamlet* is that it blurs the boundaries of two of our most basic categories – life and death. By the time the play is over, it is hard for us to tell one from the other.

Every Shakespearian tragedy involves death almost as a matter of course, as a part of the form. The tragic protagonist dies, and so do many others who get caught up, sometimes in the most peripheral way, in the action. But *Hamlet* is different. At the very outset of Macbeth's tragic course, he dismisses all thought of the life to come. For Othello, suicide in the grand tragic manner, is a natural escape, a logical and relatively easy act. For Lear, death is a deliverance, a kindness. Death is what frames the action of these plays. But in *Hamlet*, death is the picture not the frame. It is the central fact of life. Hamlet doesn't just think about death, he thinks about what it would be like to be dead. The play keeps us thinking about death all the time, about what death does to the soul and to the body. Much of the action is about the moment of death, the proper circumstances of death, the rites that should attend it, the refusal of death and life to keep their places as opposites in our categorisation of experience.

Shakespeare's is a time of random deaths, of young deaths, of mass deaths, of meaningless deaths. What Hamlet is looking for throughout the play is a meaningful death, death that is properly done, at the right time and place, death that has significance in the order of things, death that is remembered and spoken about and felt for. He is trying, in a sense, to marry his humanist understanding about the importance of every human life, the significance of humanity itself, with the obvious and inescapable fact of his world – that people die improperly, for no reason, without the true cause being known, without the proper rites being observed, without significance. If he cannot change the world he lives in, make it into one that is less dominated by death, he can at least, he believes, order the deaths that happen, make them rational. He wants to shape the old chaotic and corrupt world according to the principles of the new rationality which he has learned at Wittenberg. And of course you cannot do this; you cannot live in one world according to the principles of another world. This is what we call tragedy.

Hamlet is a man in transition from one world view to another. It is a mistake to see him entirely as an example of the New Man, as a full-blooded Renaissance intellectual. If he were, there would be no tragedy. He would not believe in the ghost, or he would use his rational faculties to tell himself that its demands are unreasonable, that they don't make sense. He would get out, go back to Wittenberg and wait for the already decaying state to fall asunder. But there is too much of the old order within himself, too much concern for its demands: he is, after all, a hereditary prince. On the one hand, we have in

Hamlet a man who believes that everything is relative, that there are no absolute standards of value or morality: 'there is nothing either good or bad but thinking makes it so'. (2, 2, 250–51) The first words of his first soliloquy have a decidedly scientific ring about them; 'melt, thaw and resolve itself into a dew'. A man who believes that there is nothing good or bad except in the way that we see it, a man who can use scientific language, is not a man who should believe in fate, who should deny free will. And yet this is what Hamlet, even the relatively cool Hamlet of the first act, does. Shakespeare gives us a Hamlet who in the course of a few lines can say on the one hand that customs should be broken ('it is a custom / More honoured in the breach than the observance'), that men should think for themselves and not be bound by what is traditional – the words of a Renaissance humanist – and then say that men are born with certain defects, that Nature or Fortune determines their characters and that there is nothing they can do about it:

> So, oft it chances in particular men
> That for some vicious mole of nature in them –
> As in their birth, wherein they are not guilty,
> Since nature cannot choose his origin,
> By the o'ergrowth of some complexion,
> Oft breaking down the pales and forts of reason,
> Or by some habit that too much o'erleavens
> The form of plausive manners – that these men
> Carrying, I say, the stamp of one defect,
> Being nature's livery, or fortune's star,

49

His virtues else, be they as pure as grace,
As infinite as man may undergo,
Shall in general censure take corruption
From that particular fault.' (1, 4, 25–)

Here, indeed, is the doctrine of the tragic flaw. But if Hamlet has a tragic flaw, it is that he can't shake off this kind of stuff.

In Shakespeare's tragedies, the real New Men, the real believers in the new philosophy, like Edmund in *King Lear*, laugh at the idea of astrology and at those who believe in it. To them, the idea of your fate and your character being determined at your birth is a foolish superstition. But Hamlet both believes it and doesn't believe it.

This is the contradictory Hamlet who takes his father's ghost's orders seriously enough to say that he doesn't care if he dies in carrying them out, and who then does not execute them. This is the Hamlet who says that theatre is a lie and then says that it can reveal the truth, the Hamlet who laughs at the idiocy of Young Fortinbras and then says that he should try to be more like him. This is the Hamlet who believes that he can deal in a world of death and yet bring order to it, the man who would try to make the irrational reasonable. It is the contradictions of his time, embodied in his own thinking, that make for Hamlet's delay, not his desire to sleep with his mother or his tragic flaw as a shirker. By accepting his duty to kill and then trying to make that killing significant in all the proper details, Hamlet is trying to keep a foot in each of two contradictory worlds, to use the ideas of one for the sordid tasks of the other. It is hardly surprising that he fails for so long.

The first argument in the play, the first clash between Hamlet and his enemies, is an argument about death. Hamlet is grieving over his father. Claudius and Gertrude believe that his mourning has gone on too long. 'How is it,' asks Claudius, 'that the clouds still hang on you?' Gertrude confronts Hamlet with a mediaeval notion of human death – that it is common, ordinary, natural, only to be expected, not something to make too much fuss over:

> Thou know'st 'tis common – all that lives must die,
> Passing through nature to eternity. (1, 2, 72–)

What Gertrude and Claudius are saying is something that reflects reality in Elizabethan England – that people die all the time, that it is no big deal. Implicit in what Gertrude says is that there is no great difference between the death of a man and the death of an animal. Her attitude is like that of the Gravemaker which will so unsettle Hamlet much later in the play: 'Custom hath made it in him a property of easiness', so that he sings while he is digging a grave. (5, 1, 67–) Both in the first and the last acts of the play, there are those to whom death is something that you just get used to.

Claudius here, though, goes further than Gertrude and stresses that death is a matter of nature taking its course and that in grieving too long Hamlet is challenging the whole feudal order, the whole sense of what is right and fitting, of an ordained way of doing things which must not be put at risk by individualistic feelings:

51

But you must know your father lost a father,
That father lost, lost his; and the survivor bound
In filial obligation for some term
To do obsequious sorrow. (1, 2, 89–)

Hamlet replies that the forms of grief, the rites that attend death, do not matter. What matters is 'that within', personal feeling. Already, in this important scene, two different ways of looking at the world, one which argues in terms of precedent and tradition – an essentially feudal view – and the other which argues in terms of personal feeling – an essentially post-feudal view – are being hammered out. And, crucially, the medium for that argument is death and what it means. We see from this early scene, which comes even before Hamlet's encounter with the Ghost, that death is to be the battleground for Hamlet's individuality. Hamlet, as we know from his long and detailed advice to the Players and the delight he takes in the whole idea of the play-within-a-play, fancies himself as a stage manager. And what he seeks to do throughout the play is to stage-manage death, to make it as significant as a work of theatre that has been rehearsed, that is performed at the right time and in the right way. It is interesting, for instance, that although Old Hamlet commands his son to 'Remember me' and Hamlet promises to do so, yet he remembers almost nothing of his living father. His conjuring of his father for Gertrude (3, 4, 54–) is a formal eulogy, a conscious performance made with a deliberate eye to its effect. But it is in marked contrast even to the warmth of his memories of his father's jester Yorick. There is no touching, intimate scene in his memory of

52

his father. What he keeps in mind, what he mulls over, what
obsesses him, is the manner of his father's death, its details and
its timing, the fact that it was unrehearsed:

> 'A took my father grossly, full of bread,
> With all his crimes broad blown, as flush as May;
> And how his audit stands, who knows save heaven?
> (3, 1, 58–)

And so he literally rehearses it, instructs his actors, has it acted
out. He tries to give to death, which throughout the play is
sudden and messy, the form and order of a work of art. He
becomes an aesthete of death from the moment he begins to
ponder his task, just as later he will be careful about specifying
the manner and timing of death even for the hapless and
insignificant Rosencrantz and Guildenstern: 'not shriving time
allowed'.

This is the significance of the 'To be or not to be' soliloquy
(3, 1, 56) and its contemplation of suicide. He talks of suicide
like a connoisseur judging a good painting. He wants to know,
not if it is morally justified, or useful, or pleasant, but
whether it is 'nobler in the mind', whether it is lofty and well-
shaped. He talks of death as a 'consummation', something
that is honed and finished and achieved. This is the significance also of Hamlet's refusal to kill Claudius in 3, 3. This
scene is generally taken as proof of the fact that Hamlet is
guilty of improper delay, that he is unable to make his mind
up to do what he ought to. His reasoning that Claudius is
praying and therefore would go to heaven if he killed him is

taken as an excuse and a very lame one. But in fact it is absolutely in keeping with the way Hamlet thinks about death throughout the play.

What he wants for Claudius's death is a kind of symmetry, an artistic harmony matching his own father's death. Old Hamlet died without having time to confess his sins; so must Claudius die. What Hamlet has done is to convince himself that he can use his own reasoning, his education in philosophy and the theatre, to make the death which he has to perform something orderly and fitting rather than something savage and belonging to the visceral irrational world of mere revenge. The death of Old Hamlet at one end of the scale will be balanced by the death in the same circumstances of Claudius at the other end. Something bloody, vicious, and dark will be made to look like something shaped, balanced, proper. The things that are not dreamt of in Horatio's philosophy will at least be managed according to that philosophy.

For Hamlet, then, the idea of death and the idea of theatre become strangely interrelated. And they are related right from the moment when the Ghost lays the burden of revenge on Hamlet. The very first thing Hamlet does after his encounter with the Ghost is to enter into an elaborate and highly theatrical ceremony of swearing, in which he takes such great delight that he keeps repeating it, somewhat to the puzzlement of Horatio and Marcellus. The idea of the ceremony strikes him suddenly and forcefully. He says that 'without more circumstance [i.e. ceremony] at all, / I hold it fit that we shake hands and part', and then a few seconds later begins to insist on his elaborate ceremonials. And it is at this moment that Shakespeare chooses one of the oddest devices of the play, a device that is there specifically to call to mind the theatre itself, to remind us that we are watching a performance of a play. When Marcellus objects to Hamlet's insistence that they swear again on his sword not to reveal the happenings of the night to anyone, the Ghost cries out 'Swear' from under the stage. His voice reminds us that there is an actor who has gone through a trapdoor under the stage, that this is a play and we have just seen a theatrical trick – the disappearance of the Ghost.

And in case we miss the point, Hamlet makes a joke to draw our attention. Hamlet has just had an awesome encounter with a terrifying ghost, the ghost of his father whom he holds in the highest respect. But what he says when he hears the 'Swear' coming from under the stage is 'Ha, ha, boy, sayest thou so? Art thou there, truepenny? / Come on. You hear this fellow in the cellarage. / Consent to swear.' 'Boy', 'truepenny', 'this fellow in the cellarage' – these are not the terms an awestruck son uses about the ghost of his dead father. They are the terms an actor uses about one of his colleagues. The actor playing Hamlet says 'Come on, you hear this old so-and-so under the floorboards, let's get on with it.' It is a joke, the kind of joke that Shakespeare often injects immediately after a scene of great solemnity and tension, but it is one which serves to remind us that the ghost we have just seen is a trick, that we are watching three actors, that this, in a sense, is a play about performance, that Hamlet is trying to stage-manage something. The connection which Hamlet makes between theatricality and the manner of death is not one that is made only in the scenes with the Players in the second act, but one which is planted in his mind at the very moment that he takes on his task of killing Claudius. At the same time, though, the effectiveness of theatricality in actually shaping or coping with reality is always ambivalent in the play. Hamlet's 'O, what a rogue and peasant slave am I!' soliloquy throws strong doubt on the relationship between theatricality and reality: the actor can put on a show of emotion and 'all for nothing'. Hamlet, though, chooses to ignore his own doubts and by the end of the same speech (2, 2, 605–6) has convinced himself that theatre can reveal the truth, that 'The play's the thing / Wherein I'll catch the conscience of the King.'

What Hamlet believes he can stage-manage, what he is most concerned with, are boundaries. He is concerned with the boundary between life and death, between this life and the next. He focuses constantly on the moment of death and how it affects the passage into the next life. He thinks about this moment, this boundary line, in relation to four separate deaths – his father's, Claudius's, Rosencrantz and Guildenstern's and his own. He believes that he can fix that line, choose the right moment of death that will determine what will happen after death. His father was killed without confession and Hamlet fears that he may be damned. Claudius he will not kill while he may be in a state of grace. Rosencrantz and Guildenstern, he specifies in his forged letter, must be killed without allowing time for confession of their sins. As for himself, he rejects suicide in the 'To be or not to be' speech precisely because it would not allow him to determine the passage he will make into death. In suicide, the afterlife would be unknown, unpredictable, 'The undiscovered country, from whose bourn no traveller returns . . .' The reason why Hamlet, by the fifth act, is prepared to face his end, is that he believes that he knows the boundary, that the passage will be significant, providential, artistically shaped. He can tell Horatio that 'There's a special providence in the fall of a sparrow. If it be now, 'tis not to come; if it be not to come, it will be now; if it be not now, yet it will come. The readiness is all.' (5, 2, 165–) He is ready for his death, he has rehearsed it, it will be all right on the night.

4. Crossing the Line

Hamlet's tragedy is that he is wrong about his ability to fix the boundaries of life and death. He says that death is a country from which 'no traveller returns' but he should know that this is not so, for he has already seen his father return from death. Throughout the play, the categories of life and death refuse to hold. They seep into each other, constantly blur their boundaries, so that Hamlet's belief that the boundary can be fixed and achieved becomes impossible. Right from the start of the play, the rites by which we separate life from death, the rituals of funeral and burial, have been disrupted and are failing to function properly. Claudius's first speech (1, 2) is about the way in which the rituals of life and those of death have been mixed up and his language mirrors the uncomfortable contradiction, yoking together opposites in an uneasy alliance:

> . . . as 'twere with a defeated joy,
> With one auspicious and one dropping eye
> With mirth in funeral and with dirge in marriage,

And, as the play goes on, those rites break down completely. The dead Polonius, in the fourth act, is denied his proper funeral ('we have done but greenly,' says Claudius, 'in hugger-mugger to inter him;'). The dead Ophelia in the fifth act is given the truncated funeral rites that cause Laertes to ask repeatedly 'What ceremony else?'

> We should profane the service of the dead
> To sing sage requiem and such rest to her
> As to peace-parted souls. (5, 1, 231–)

And finally the graveyard itself is desecrated by Hamlet and Laertes fighting in it, trying to kill each other in an open grave, the ultimate symbol of burial without the proper rituals. The public rites which mark the passage between life and death have collapsed completely.

But it is not just the rituals marking the boundaries of life and death which refuse to hold. In the very imaginations of the characters, the distinction between the two keeps getting blurred. Hamlet himself can hardly think of a dead person without imagining him alive. When he has just killed Polonius he imagines him as he was when he was alive and proceeds to talk to him in exactly the same sarcastic way we have seen him use earlier.

> This counsellor
> Is now most still, most secret, and most grave,
> Who was in life a foolish prating knave.
> Come, sir, to draw toward an end with you. (3, 4, 187–)

The very pun on 'grave' sums up the blurring of life and death, for it is both an attribute of a living person and a symbol of death. Hamlet is always resurrecting the dead. His father is reborn in his son's eulogies of him. He resurrects the dead Ophelia as an object of love after he has spurned the living woman. And, of course, in the scene with Yorick's skull, he brings his father's dead jester back to life.

This, indeed, is the point of the Yorick scene. (5, 1, 176–) There is probably no scene in any play ever written that has become so much of a cliché and that has suffered so much as a consequence. Hamlet, looking at the skull, is not staring into the emptiness of death. Rather he is filling that emptiness, bringing it back to life, recreating Yorick with a warmth and humanity that are in marked contrast to the beautiful but lifeless eulogy of his own dead father. In this speech, the living and the dead mingle with a startling intimacy. The dead man's skull had lips that Hamlet kissed. He played tricks, gave piggyback rides. He sang, tumbled, told jokes. What we get is not a speech about the futility of life, but a speech about the wonder of life, about how much is lost in death. Looking at a rotten and smelly skull, Hamlet can give us a sense of the sadness of death which he and the court of Elsinore cannot manage for any of the real deaths which take place within the play.

Here, the borders of life and death have been completely broken. Just as at the start of the play Claudius remembers the mixture of wedding and funeral, so here Hamlet creates a sense of madcap fun in a graveyard, invoking a feast that reminds us of the earlier wedding feast ('your flashes of merriment that were wont to set the table on a roar'). The Gravedigger adds to the scene's blurring of the distinction between life and death. When Hamlet asks him how long it will take a man to rot in the grave, the Gravedigger immediately thinks of living people who are already like dead ones – 'if 'a be not rotten before 'a die' – and goes on to conjure up the image of a living man, a tanner, at his trade. He then talks of water decaying dead bodies, which reminds us immediately of a live body – Ophelia – whose destruction by water has just been evoked. All the time in the scene the distinction between the living and the dead is being broken down.

And this, too, is the cause of Hamlet's pain. For in looking at death and invoking life, Hamlet invokes sex. Throughout the play sex is the essence of life, but as life becomes mixed up with death, so sex becomes mixed up with death. Even before he meets the Ghost, Hamlet's torment has come from the mixture of sex and death – his father's death and his mother's wedding. Looking at Yorick's skull, he cannot help but think of a woman in her bedroom: 'Now get you to my lady's chamber, and tell her, let her paint an inch thick, to this favour she must come.'

And this is true throughout the play. In one of the play's most shocking images, the 'mad' Hamlet, talking to Polonius, mixes sexual generation with death, and both with Ophelia: 'if the sun breed maggots in a dead dog, being a good kissing carrion – have you a daughter?' (2, 2, 183–) Death becomes birth and the whole is mixed up with his own desire for Ophelia. And in the play's imagery, maggots themselves, the life that is being born from the dead dog, are connected back to death: 'We fat ourselves for maggots'. (4, 3, 23)

Sex and death become enmeshed even in the flowers that Ophelia is carrying in her own mad scene. Gertrude talks of the 'long purples', flowers that 'liberal shepherds give a grosser name / But our cold maids do dead men's fingers call them.' (4, 7, 141–) The same flower, in the shepherds' rude name, can be associated with sex, or it can, in the name the maids give it, be associated with dead bodies.

It is important to remember that this confusion of sex and death is not primarily psychological. It does not come about because Hamlet wants to sleep with his mother, or with a dead dog, or even with a maggot. It comes from the blurring of distinctions, of rigid categories, which is rooted in the play's place at a point of transition between one world view and another. We are not shown it as an internal process, something happening in Hamlet's soul or subconscious. We encounter it as a public phenomenon, something that is connected to the breakdown of institutions and indeed of the entire state of Denmark. For just as the public rituals which separate life from death – the funerals and burials – break down in the course of the play, so too do the public institutions that contain sexual life – the family, the very distinction between men and women.

What happens to Ophelia when her father dies and she goes mad is that she begins to confuse her father with her would-be lover, Hamlet. A dead man is confused with a living man and that confusion of life and death becomes a confusion of sexual and familial roles. Her song of mourning (4, 5, 23) is for her 'true love', who is 'dead and gone', but, of course, it is not her true love (Hamlet) who is dead, but her father. And she also confuses men and women. When she is leaving, she says 'sweet ladies, good night, good night', though two of the three people she is talking to are men. And when she returns later in the scene, she again confuses father and lover in her song, this time more explicitly: 'It is the false steward that stole his master's daughter.' In reality, her grief concerns the false master (Hamlet) that did not steal his steward's daughter (Ophelia). Laertes understands that there is meaning in this seeming distraction: 'This nothing's more than matter.' (4, 5, 171–)

In all of this, Ophelia is only following Hamlet himself, and in particular what Hamlet has done to her. The mocking Hamlet, horrified by the confusion of sexual roles implicit in his mother marrying her husband's brother, takes up this confusion of sexual roles and sexual identity. On leaving for England he calls to Claudius 'Farewell, dear mother.' When Claudius corrects him, he enjoys himself with the way in which, in Elsinore, sexual categories have ceased to have any meaning: 'My mother – father and mother is man and wife, man and wife is one flesh, and so, my mother.' (4, 3, 50–) But this confusion of sexual categories is far from funny in what he has already done to Ophelia. Ophelia, in her 'mad' confusion of father and lover, is only repeating Hamlet's confusion of mother and lover in his cruel attack on her fragile identity. Hamlet's baiting of Ophelia in 3, 1, comes shortly before his confrontation with his mother in 3, 4 and it is a rehearsal for that confrontation. It is Hamlet being the stage manager, trying out the power of his words to turn into daggers. The charge he lays against Orphelia – lustfulness and sexual inconstancy – is the accusation he wants to make against his mother. He uses her as a substitute for his mother, deprives her of her proper category. And something deprived of its proper category, of its place in the catalogue, can easily get lost. This is what happens to Ophelia.

Shakespeare has shown us an Ophelia who is shaped and formed and defined by others, in particular by men. She is defined in turn by Laertes, Polonius, and Hamlet and deserted in turn by each. She has no identity of her own, only that which is constructed for her by others. In 1, 3 she replies to Polonius's question as to what she should think with 'I do not know, my lord, what I should think.' Subsequently she replies to Hamlet's similar question as to her thoughts: 'I think nothing, my lord.' All her actions and responses are about what other people think for her and of her before they disappear and her defining forces are removed.

Ophelia is the play's image of what happens when things and people become undefined, when set categories refuse to hold their place. The problem for Hamlet is that even while the distinction between life and death is falling apart in the most intimate of ways throughout the play, he still maintains the belief that he can manipulate that distinction, that he can pin-point the boundary between life and death and use it to his own ends. In this he is terribly wrong. The action of the play itself, as it gathers force, makes this abundantly clear to us. Hamlet says that he will 'defy augury' but this is untrue because there is a building pattern of prophecy in the play which turns out to be true.

The play has premonitions of death, areas in which the dis-tinction between life and death breaks down to such a degree that the living already appear to be dead. Ophelia mourns her dead lover (Hamlet) while Hamlet is still alive. Hamlet talks of dead kings – Alexander, Caesar – and then says 'Here comes the king' (5, 1, 204), prefiguring the death of the living Claudius by associating him with the dead. And, most starkly, both Hamlet and Laertes, who are to die together, jump into the same open grave. Hamlet's belief that life and death will keep their places is being contradicted throughout the final acts by what we see and hear.

What motivates Hamlet throughout the play is his belief that death can be made orderly, can be made rational, can, in fact, become a solution. And he sees it as a solution not just to his own troubles, but to the troubles and injustices of the wider world. The 'To be or not to be' speech in which he considers the benefits of suicide, far from being the speech of an isolated neurotic, is the speech of a man with a keen political sense and a sharp social knowledge. Its imagery is full of the reality of a corrupt world – oppression, the arrogance of the powerful, the malfunctioning of the law. To its images of injustice are added images of hard labour, of grunting and sweating under heavy loads. It is an extraordinary speech to come from a prince of the realm, a full and terrible picture of social inequality. Clearly, that inequality and injustice weigh on Hamlet's mind, and we know from what Claudius says that Hamlet is popular with the mob, with the same people who come to the door with Laertes looking for the world to be made new.

And it is precisely as a vehicle for equality that Hamlet is attracted to death. On the one hand, by matching Claudius's death with that of Old Hamlet, he can make things equal in that respect. And on the other hand, he views death as a more general leveller, as that which makes social divisions equal. 'Your fat king and your lean beggar is but variable service – two dishes, but to one table.' (4, 3, 23–) Or, 'a king may go a progress through the guts of a beggar.' (4, 3, 30–) And in one of the more complicated set of images in the play, he brings these two senses of equality together – his own struggle with Claudius and the general equalisation of social distinctions. He uses images of fishing in 4, 2 and in 5, 1, comparing himself to a fish and Claudius to an angler ('Thrown out his angle for my proper life'), and he also sees the man fishing with a worm which has eaten the dead body of a king as the ultimate proof of human equality: 'A man may fish with the worm that hath eat of a king and eat of the fish that hath fed of that worm.' Far from contemplating death as mere non-existence, Shakespeare has Hamlet draw on the powerful radical tradition of using death – 'Death the Leveller' – as an image for the dissolution of social classes. Death, the very thing which Hamlet believes can define boundaries in the play, can bring order and shape to things that have gone awry, is also being used as an image of the breaking of boundaries. In this double-action is the real tragedy of *Hamlet*.

For the thing about Hamlet's attempts to stage-manage a death that will be orderly, well-formed, and, above all, meaningful is that it goes horribly wrong, is mocked at every turn by the action of the play and in particular by Hamlet's own actions. He kills Polonius by mistake, in a sordid, meaningless way and ends up having to 'lug the guts into the neighbour room' (3, 4, 186) and hide the body without ceremony, without justice, without any sense of rightness or balance. This is why his reaction on discovering that the person he has killed is Polonius and not Claudius is one, not of horror, sorrow or remorse, as we might expect from a sensitive man, but one of anger. He immediately begins to berate the corpse, like a director berating an actor who has wandered on in the wrong scene and spoiled his effects. And again, when his actions lead to the death of Ophelia, his reaction to her funeral in the graveyard is a petulant one, that of an actor who has been upstaged, demanding his rightful place in the action over lesser actors like Laertes.

His last throw of the dice is on his own death. The scene in which Hamlet, Laertes, Gertrude and Claudius die is in itself almost a play-within-a-play. It is a formal show organized before a court audience, with all the ceremonies that should attach to such a formal performance. It harks back both to the scene with the Players and to the earlier elaborate ceremony of swearing over Hamlet's sword. It is pure theatre, with all the appropriate props – the poisoned cup and the poisoned sword, the trumpet blasts, even the applause of an appreciative crowd – of a big theatrical death scene. But far from being inevitable, far from us having the sense of a fated event working its way out, it is a shambles. It is a mess. It is all about 'purposes mistook fall'n on th' inventors' heads'. Hamlet cannot even kill Claudius cleanly and singly. He has to, as it were, kill him twice, with poison and with stabbing. The single act which should balance out everything becomes double. Nothing will work out as it should, nothing will stick to its place in the script.

And even then, what is on Hamlet's mind? He wants his story to be told, he wants his life and death to be given the shape and significance of a work of art: 'And in this harsh world draw thy breath in pain, / To tell my story.' He still believes that his death, in the midst of all of these 'casual slaughters' can be individual, can have significance and shape. He dies. The play is over. Hamlet will be remembered. He will have given to at least one death in this succession of deaths a meaning. Horatio speaks a loving and lovely lullaby: 'Good night, sweet prince, / And flights of angels sing thee to thy rest.' But the play is not over. Drums beat. An Ambassador enters, someone we have not seen before in the play. What does he have to say? 'That Rosencrantz and Guildenstern are dead.' He comes to announce, at the moment when Hamlet seems to have at last given to death some significance, a completely insignificant set of deaths, utterly without meaning, wandering in from another part of the play, a couple of minor players staggering onstage at the climax to upstage the star. The play itself should be over but refuses to close. Even with his death, Hamlet has achieved nothing. We are in a truly tragic world, left with only the straw man, the man who will die for a straw and is puffed up with ambition, who will countenance 'The imminent death of twenty thousand men' for the sake of 'a fantasy and trick of fame'. Fortinbras, the man who sends thousands to the slaughter for no good reason, is hardly someone to make a single, individual death meaningful. He is the ultimate image of Hamlet's failure.

3

Othello: Inside Out

1. Is Othello Stupid?

If you look at the character of Othello in isolation, and in particular if you look at him through the notion of the 'tragic flaw', then he is not, for all his facility with words, very bright. He can talk up a storm, but he's not much for thinking. His tragic flaw is jealousy and he carries it around like a crutch, just waiting for someone to kick it from under him. He is manipulated by Iago, a man he didn't even trust enough in the first place to make him his lieutenant, without ever attempting to ascertain facts for himself. Suspecting his wife, he fails to confront her with her supposed infidelity, or to question her alleged lover, or to ask any of the other people who could tell him what's going on. He is driven demented by a handkerchief. He is not tragic, merely pathetic.

As it happens, there is no play in which Shakespeare is less interested in 'character' or in the isolated hero than *Othello*. To take character first, Shakespeare is so little interested in character in *Othello*, that some of the characters simply don't add up. Take Cassio, for instance. After Othello, Iago and Desdemona, his is the most important role in the play. He is the supposed lover of Desdemona, the cause of the tragic ending. He is also the person who is to be left to clean up the mess, replacing the dead Othello as Governor of Cyprus. Yet basic things about him and his relationship to Othello are utterly inconsistent.

In the first act, he is said to be a man 'almost damned in a fair wife' (1, 1, 20), but in the last three acts he is a sexually active bachelor. In the first act, he doesn't know about Othello and Desdemona. 'I do not understand,' he says when Iago tells him that Othello has married. (1, 2, 52) In the third act, though, Desdemona says to Othello that Cassio 'came a-wooing with you' (3, 3, 72) and Othello himself says that Cassio knew of their love 'from first to last'. (3, 3, 98) Is he married or not? Has he been Othello's intimate, trusted friend or not? If Cassio's character were of the slightest importance, Shakespeare would at least have made his mind up about such things.

Or take Roderigo, Iago's first dupe. How well does he know Desdemona whom he lusts after for so long? Very well in the first act. He has often been an unwelcome guest in her father's house, and she is probably sick of the sight of him. Yet in the fourth act, he is threatening Iago that 'I will make myself known to Desdemona.' (4, 2, 201) And both this and the

70

inconsistencies about Cassio, while they were hardly deliberate on Shakespeare's part, were clearly considered unimportant by him. We know that he revised the play carefully: clearly, having consistent characters wasn't one of his major concerns.

More importantly, Othello simply cannot be considered in isolation from Iago. There is no Othello without Iago: it is Iago who draws out his inner fears and longings, who makes him the character that we see and hear. And the tragedy is not just Othello's, it is also Iago's. Iago is as much a tragic figure as any of Shakespeare's protagonists, as much caught between one world and another, one way of thinking and another. If Iago were given another speech or two at the end of the play, the title could be changed from *Othello* to *Iago*, for everything else makes Iago fit for the role of protagonist. He has the soliloquies. He is the one who most reveals himself to the audience. He is the most active character in the play. (Othello, for a hero, is strikingly passive. Hamlet, who is regarded as the archetypal shirker, fights pirates, boards ships, deals with ghosts, directs a play, kills people, has rows in graveyards. Othello suffers, kills and dies.) And Iago also has the longest part, not merely the longest in *Othello* but the longest part in all of Shakespeare. To see the play as being about a tragic hero called Othello is absurd.

And Othello, anyway, is not a tragic hero in any classical sense. In the first place, he is not a king or a prince or a ruler, as Lear, Caesar, Anthony and Cleopatra, Hamlet, Coriolanus and Macbeth are. And because of this, his personal tragedy does not involve the tearing apart of the state or the order of nature or the universe. On the contrary, he is a servant – a highly important servant, admittedly, but a servant nonetheless. His role is dependent on the state's need for him, and he knows it: 'I have done the state some service.' (5, 2, 348) The 'other world' is not involved: there are no ghosts or witches and there is no pattern of images creating an imagined universe. His story involves battles and a general threat to the stability of the state, but they are there only to be forgotten, to become irrelevant in the context of the emotional battle that he has to fight with himself.

The world will not be corrupted by his misdeeds and we, as an audience, do not feel that there is anything necessary or significant, never mind inevitable, about his death. On the contrary, it is an adjunct to a terrible mistake, an afterthought to an error. And because the whole world has not been involved in his tragedy, because it is so intensely personal, the tragedy of a victim rather than an active controller of other people's lives, there is no need to restore the social and political order in the end. It has not been destroyed.

This is not to say, though, that there are not great forces whirling around this intimate and intense story of a man and a woman and what can be done to them. In the first place, it is not for nothing that Shakespeare uses the setting of Venice. For Venice, to an Elizabethan or Jacobean audience was a byword for new money, for the new unscrupulous capitalism that was successfully challenging the old European feudal powers. Setting a play in Venice in Shakespeare's time was like setting one on Wall Street now. It told the audience that the context for the action was money, commerce, dynamic capitalism.

What is especially interesting about Venice as a setting for the play, though, is not just that it has this single obvious meaning for a contemporary audience, but that it has a double meaning. As we have seen, Shakespeare's tragedies are concerned with things becoming double, having no fixed single meaning, with opposites melting into each other and things breaking through the definitions that we expect of them. And so it is with Venice for Shakespeare and his audience. Venice is on the one hand a shorthand name for vigorous capitalism and its ability to break through boundaries and mix up things which had previously been well-defined, a racial and religious melting pot looking with one eye towards the Christian civilization of the West and with the other towards the Islamic infidels of the East. Shakespeare himself had already used Venice in this precise sense five years before he wrote *Othello*, in *The Merchant of Venice*.

But on the other hand, Venice is also a byword for exotic vices and unbridled passions, a part of the Italian vogue, the craze for setting plays in Italy which had been raging since the end of the sixteenth century in the English theatre. In this competing stereotype, it was the land of the atheistic, amoral political theorist, Machiavelli, of intriguing intrigues and perfidious poisoners. It was a place full of tight political plots and loose women. Around 1599 English playwrights discovered that they could write about corrupt courts, cynical rulers, religious leaders who preached purity and practised promiscuity, and society ladies who treated their hankies with more care than their wedding vows. They could do all of these things without getting hanged, drawn and quartered – provided they set such plays in exotic Italy, so different, of course, from our own dear sceptred isle.

Faced with this choice of connotations for his chosen setting, Shakespeare typically uses both. It is essential to the story that Venice, dynamic, open and unbound by feudal traditions, allows a man of the 'wrong' colour and of no social standing in a Christian republic, to become an important figure in the state. Othello's ascent from actually being a slave (1, 3, 137) to being entrusted with the security of one of the world's great trading powers, is a kind of social mobility, based solely on his skills as a soldier, that was a new, tenuous possibility in Elizabethan England, and absolutely unthinkable in any feudal society.

Venice is a place where black and white are literally no longer opposites, where pragmatic, commercial values are threatening what would previously have been absolute distinctions. And it is interesting that no Venetian, even Othello's deadliest enemies, however racist they may be, ever suggests that a black outsider should not be allowed to lead the Venetian forces. Everyone accepts that he is the best man for the job, even those who are so bigoted that the sight of Othello's black skin makes them want to throw up. There is a meritocracy at work that is so strong that it forms a good part of Iago's hatred of Othello.

At the same time, though, Shakespeare also makes use of the second stereotype. Iago, most obviously, is a version of the Machiavellian villain, though one who grows to a complexity well beyond his origins. The undisguised sexuality which runs through the play is made possible by its exotic setting. The quickness with which the characters are roused to passions of all sorts is a way of using the Italian stereotype. And, of course, the assumption running through the play that infidelity in women is the norm rather than the exception depends upon the same association of Italy with sexual vice.

The doubleness of these connotations of the setting in Venice – dynamism and decadence, openness and intrigue, commercial virility and sexual vice – is reinforced by the fact that the play both is and is not set in Venice. It opens in Venice, is essentially bound up with the city all the way through, but moves after the first act to the never-never land of Cyprus. Shakespeare makes use of the free state, the new money and the new man, but at a distance, giving himself room for ambivalence about its force and its consequences. If the context begins as the great force in history which Venice represents – broadly, the replacement of feudalism by capitalism – that context narrows as the play goes on to the war within an intimately connected set of minds. The war doesn't make sense without the greater context, but it has its own dynamics, the byzantine tensions of sex and race. For *Othello* is the story of the way in which external things – politics, culture, prejudices – become internal, become part of the most intimate details of a man's thoughts and feelings.

2. Black and Tan

The most obvious thing about Othello has also been, in the way that the play has been taught and interpreted, the least obvious. Othello is black, but Othello, a man who engages our sympathies more immediately and more directly than any other Shakespearian tragic protagonist, could not, in a long tradition of criticism of the play, possibly be black. How could a black man be so noble, so engaging, so obviously capable of such delicacy of feeling? There are two ways of dealing with this. One is to deny that Othello's blackness has anything much to do with the play. The other, by the vehemence with which it insists that Othello could not really be played as black on the stage, disproves the first, showing by its very racism the centrality of the colour of Othello's skin to the play as a whole.

Even at the end of the century in which *Othello* was written, Thomas Rymer found it utterly implausible: a 'blackamoor' could not have risen to be anything higher than a trumpeter and could not have married a woman other than 'some little drab'. All of the most important critics of the nineteenth century, the time when so much of what we take to be accepted wisdom about Shakespeare's tragedies was laid down, are creepily racist about *Othello*. Coleridge says that we should make the best of a bad job and play Othello as merely brown, for, 'It would be something monstrous to conceive this beautiful Venetian girl falling in love with a veritable Negro.' Charles Lamb, in a wild fit of tolerance, suggests that perhaps Desdemona is not 'altogether to be condemned for the unsuitableness of the person whom she selected as her lover'. A. C. Bradley feels that it would be better to play Othello as tanned rather than really black, since otherwise a civilized audience would be disgusted at the sight of him:

'perhaps if we saw Othello coal-black with the bodily eye the aversion of our blood, an aversion which comes as near to being merely physical as anything human can, would over-power our imagination . . .'

It would, of course, be equally outrageous to see *Othello* as a play about racism in a modern sense. Shakespeare's England was not a multi-racial society or the centre of a multi-racial Empire as it would later become. At the same time, though, Shakespeare was certainly conscious of race. If there was no large black population in his England, there were significant numbers of black people, significant enough for Queen Elizabeth to complain in 1601 of being 'discontented at the great numbers of Negars and blackamoors which are crept into the realm'. And we know that Shakespeare was aware of the fear, revulsion and sexual disgust which blackness could invoke in a contemporary audience because he used it quite frequently. Portia in *The Merchant of Venice* is glad to be rid of the Prince of Morocco and 'all of his complexion'. The King of Naples in *The Tempest* is criticized for having married his daughter to the King of Tunis even though the court had pleaded with him not to 'loose her to an African'. Hamlet talks of his mother's desire to 'batten on this Moor', a pun in which 'Moor' is used as the opposite of 'fair'. Aaron the Moor in *Titus Andronicus* is an atheist and an 'inhuman dog'. What is unusual about *Othello* then, is not that it uses racial antagonisms, but the attitude it adopts towards them. For if, in *Titus Andronicus*, it is the Moor who is an 'inhuman dog', in *Othello* it is not the Moor, but his tormentor Iago, who is described as an 'inhuman dog'. (5, 1, 64)

Far from being an incidental detail, the imagery, and even the structure of the play, emphasize the importance of blackness and whiteness, darkness and light, to its effect. The blonde Desdemona's virtue, for example, is to be turned to black pitch by Iago's schemes. The first act and the last act take place in a darkness that is pierced by light, making the contrast, and the intermingling of one with the other, visibly present on stage.

In the first act, the torches of the various groups who rush about the streets of Venice light up the darkness, and Brabantio specifically links these torches in the night with the marriage of the black Othello to his own white daughter:

> Belief of it oppresses me already.
> Light, I say, light! (1, 1, 142–)

And this beginning is balanced by the visual imagery of the ending, with the play's last scene being set in motion by Othello entering the darkness with a light, a light which he again explicitly links to Desdemona's whiteness: 'Put out the light [i.e. the lamp] and then put out the light [i.e. Desdemona].' (5, 2, 7) The play is literally framed by its imagery of black and white.

And at a deeper, psychological level, blackness, or rather the white man's fear of blackness, fuels much of the play's imagery. If the political context of racism has changed since the time that Shakespeare wrote *Othello*, the psychological context has changed remarkably little, and it is this which gives the play its continuing urgency. Exactly the same mixture of fear and sexual fascination, of a sense of inadequacy that turns into a sense of superiority, still applies 400 years later. The racist Iago constantly links Othello's blackness to animality, comparing his sexuality, for instance, to that of a horse: 'You'll have your daughter covered with a Barbary horse, you'll have your nephews neigh to you, you'll have coursers for cousins, and gennets for germans.' (1, 1, 113–)

In our own time, this tendency, at once contemptuous and sexually fearful, continues in the white mind. The black psychologist Franz Fanon remarked on how 'The negro symbolises the biological . . . I have always been struck by the speed with which "handsome young Negro" turns into "young colt" or "stallion".' Fanon found that sixty per cent of white Europeans whom he questioned associated the word 'Negro' with 'boxer, biology, penis, strong, athletic, savage, animal, devil, sin'. To those around him Othello also brings these images to mind. He is 'warlike Othello' (strong, athletic, savage); 'an old black ram' (an image of both the animal and the sexual); he is a 'blacker devil'. The response to Othello in the play is still the response of many whites to the black man, and the fact that the imagery is unchanged over the centuries shows how deeply Shakespeare connects with the psychology of racism.

The important thing, indeed the crucial thing, for an understanding of what happens in the play, though, is that this racism isn't just the context in which Othello lives. It has entered his mind and his soul. It is an integral part of him, a piece of the outside world which he carries around in his most intimate, private self. It is the connection between the world around him and his thoughts, desires, feelings. Iago is able to influence Othello, not because Othello is stupid, or because he carries jealousy like an original sin stamped on his soul, but because Iago makes this connection. Iago's brilliance lies not in what he puts into Othello's mind, but what he draws out of it. He takes what is already there, and gives it 'a local habitation and a name', takes shame and doubt and gives them visible substance.

As soon as he starts to believe that Desdemona may be unfaithful to him, Othello blames the colour of his own skin. 'Haply for I am black . . . She's gone.' (3, 3, 267–) It is the first explanation he thinks of. Iago is able to undermine Othello's confidence in his wife only because Othello himself cannot suppress the idea within his own mind that Desdemona must be strange and wilful in her tastes to have married him in the first place. Iago plays on Othello's self-contempt, on the innate sense of inferiority which he has absorbed from the racism all around him. Marrying Desdemona may have proved Othello worthy of white love, respect and admiration, but it has not made him white. The very sense of triumph with which he talks of his marriage, his conversion of it into a military manoeuvre with Desdemona as his 'fair warrior', shows his need for that acceptance, a need that makes him continually vulnerable to Iago's promptings. He projects that insecurity on to Desdemona – if he is unworthy of her love, then she must be perverse for loving him, and if she is perverse, then she must be unfaithful. He accepts without question Iago's suggestion that Desdemona must be unnatural for having preferred Othello to 'many proposed matches / Of her own clime, complexion, and degree'. (3, 3, 234–35) What he hates when he hates her is himself, the image of his own blackness which he sees in her disgrace:

> My name, that was as fresh
> As Dian's visage, is now begrimed and black
> As mine own face. (3, 3, 391–)

In her supposed infidelity, he sees the part of himself that he has been taught to despise, the colour of his skin.

3. Under the Skin

Iago understands Othello, knows how to draw out what is dormant in his general's mind, because he shares his fears and his shame. Othello comes to believe that he is being cuckolded because, at some level, he feels he should be cuckolded. Iago has precisely the same feeling. In this, as in so much else, Iago and Othello are brothers under the skin.

Iago is so filled with sexual disgust and hatred of women that he cannot think of either sex or women without thinking of animals. From the first scene of the play onwards, he habitually thinks of lovers as animals, Othello as a ram, Desdemona a ewe: 'an old black ram / Is tupping your white ewe.' (1, 1, 88–89) Making love is making 'the beast with two backs'. (1, 1, 118) Othello, is a Barbary horse, Desdemona, when she is not a lifeless object like a treasure ship (1, 2, 50), is, like all women, a kind of animal, a wild cat or a guinea hen. A married man is a yoked beast of burden. He himself is a spider, Cassio a fly (2, 1, 171), Roderigo a hunting dog (2, 1, 303). He cannot think of sex, or, as the play goes on, of anything else, without draining it of its humanity, making it into something either mechanical or animal.

And the remarkable thing about this disgust is that it is very like Othello's self-disgust. Iago, the cool tormentor of Othello with visions of his wife's adultery, also torments himself with visions of his own wife's adultery. While playing on the self-contempt that allows Othello to believe that Desdemona should be betraying him, Iago is himself prey to the same delusion. And it is a mark of how closely he identifies with Othello that he, Othello's tormentor, imagines Othello to be his tormentor. According to Emilia, Iago has long suspected her 'with the Moor'. (4, 2, 151) Earlier Iago himself has told Othello that 'knowing what I am, I know what she shall be' (4, 1, 72), meaning that since he himself is a cuckold, he knows that women must be unfaithful. It is a telling phrase, moving as it does from his view of himself to his view of humanity. Like Othello, he moves from the inside out, not from the external world of evidence to the internal world of conviction.

This identification of himself with Othello goes even further in his imagery and in his positioning within the play. In the structure of the play, as we have seen, Othello's blackness and the blackness of the night are identified. Yet it is Iago who makes darkness his proper element, taking the blackness of Othello on to himself. It is he who dominates the three night scenes (1, 1; 2, 3; and 5, 1). And, in a play in which Othello is identified with the Devil, Iago is at pains to take that identification on himself. At every hand's turn he calls on the powers of blackness ('When devils do the blackest sins put on . . .' 2, 3, 342), and believes that he can turn white to black, Desdemona's virtue 'into pitch'. (2, 3, 351) The words he uses and the parts of the play he uses them in are calculated to identify Iago with Othello.

So close are Iago and Othello, indeed, that they start to melt into each other. Not only does Iago take on Othello's association with blackness, but Othello starts to take on Iago's characteristic imagery and style of speech. In the early part of the play, Iago and Othello speak differently, not only in the obvious sense that Iago uses much more prose than Othello does, but also in the contrast between Iago's blunt and often coarse style and Othello's stately and deliberate poetic speech. But in the last two acts, as the two minds begin to fuse together, as Iago's words give shape to Othello's thoughts, so Othello starts to sound more and more like Iago.

Like Iago, he starts to turn people into animals in his imagery, conjuring up a world of goats, monkeys, toads, crocodiles, blood-sucking flies and poisonous snakes. Like Iago, he starts to appeal to the devil and fill his speech with diabolic images of Desdemona as 'fair devil', 'false as hell', 'double damned', their bedroom as hell itself. This switching of styles of speech, in which the borders of individual character become completely permeable is at its most dramatic in 4, 1, when Othello is finally persuaded by Iago that Desdemona is unfaithful. Othello's grand verse breaks down into jagged, disordered prose. Iago's prose becomes triumphant verse. The two men are so interlocked that it is impossible to tell them completely apart.

But why does Iago make this destructive identification with Othello? The source of Othello's self-contempt may be his position as a black man in a white society, but what is the source of Iago's? Here again, Iago is a reverse mirror-image of Othello. Othello suffers the uncertainties of having benefited from a new openness in society, a new possibility for a man to achieve high office without social standing. Iago suffers from the precise reverse, from the uncertainties of being wedded to order, degree, a sense of each thing being in its place, in a world where all of these things are being swept away. And Othello is the embodiment of these forces, the living proof of the way in which old distinctions are breaking down. Iago suffers directly from this breakdown, by being denied his place as Othello's lieutenant.

Iago is as close to being a tragic protagonist as makes no real difference. He is closer to a Lear, a Hamlet or a Macbeth than Othello is. Like them, he is caught between an old world and a new one, a medieval set of values and a modern one. Hamlet tries to order an old world, a world of duty and revenge, by new methods, those of the new humanist philosophy. Iago tries to restore an old world, that of order, degree, hierarchy, by new methods, those of ruthless, cynical rationality. He is caught in an impossible contradiction, using injustice to restore justice, lies to restore the truth, a convoluted disorder to create a simple order. In doing so he constitutes a critique of both the old world and the new, his psychotic sense of order discrediting the very notion of order, his perverted rationality destroying the very notion of reason.

Iago explains his immediate motivation right at the start of the play, in his first long harangue to Roderigo. His complaint is that now, in these new times, a man is no longer valued by his position in the hierarchy, his place in the social queue:

> Preferment goes by letter and affection,
> And not by the old gradation, where each second
> Stood heir to th' first. (1, 1, 36–)

It is the collapse of feudalism in a nutshell, the replacement of a system built on knowing one's place, 'the old gradation', by a more mobile and flexible one. Iago should have inherited the job of lieutenant. Instead, it has gone to Cassio. And Iago's description of Cassio broadens the base of his attack to take in the whole new world, its concerns with money and business on the one hand and its new scientific ideology on the other. Cassio, Iago tells us, is an 'arithmetician', a 'Florentine' (Florence being famed for its bankers and accountants), a 'debitor and creditor' (i.e. a book-keeper), a 'counter-caster' (i.e. a petty accountant). From the one slight to himself, he builds an assault on the whole rising order of society.

And this assault is deepened as the play goes on, becoming fundamental and philosophical. In his lecture to Roderigo in the third scene, he gives his vision of human order and balance, an essentially medieval order in which everything is balanced by everything else, in which emotional forces are kept in their place by reason, and reason by emotions: 'If the balance of our lives had not one scale of reason to poise another of sensuality, the blood and baseness of our natures would conduct us to most preposterous conclusions. But we have reason to cool our raging motions . . .' (1, 3, 319–) This is Iago's guiding principle, but, in dramatic terms, it is already deeply ironic. For this classical vision of the golden mean, of harmony in human conduct, is expounded as part of Iago's plan to dupe Roderigo. It is reason in the service of cynical barbarity, Iago in a nutshell.

This demented use of harmony, balance and order to achieve something violent, cruel and inhuman reaches its climax in Iago's scenario for Desdemona's death. Having used the business with the handkerchief to finally convince Othello of Desdemona's treachery, Iago goes on to dictate the manner of her killing. Othello suggests poison, but Iago insists that she should be strangled in the marriage bed. This is objectively against Iago's interests, since Desdemona could be poisoned quietly, without being given the chance to dissuade Othello, whereas strangulation means that Othello has to confront her, risking that 'her body and beauty unprovide my mind again'. (4, 1, 200) But Iago insists on it out of his perverse sense of balance and justice. She has, supposedly, sinned against the marriage bed, therefore she must be punished there: 'strangle her in her bed, even the bed she hath contaminated.' (4, 1, 202) This is the 'old gradation' restored, everything put back in its proper place.

Iago's lunatic sense of order is itself an implicit criticism of the old order, but the play has more explicit things to say about it as well. The whole idea of duty, not as something sickeningly simple in Iago's obsessive sense, but as something complex and double-edged, is introduced early on in the play. Duty, indeed, is one of those things that gets split, becomes divided, in a typically Shakespearean way here. Desdemona, in a scene that Shakespeare would repeat in *King Lear* and that therefore had particular meaning for Shakespeare around this time, talks of her 'divided duty'. Like Cordelia in *King Lear*, she has duties to her father and to her husband, and the two are incompatible. (1, 3, 179–187) Duty is not absolute, but contingent on human needs and desires. The old order, Iago's gradation, has its place, but only so long as it can be accommodated to the proper demands of real people. It is this human factor that Iago leaves out of account.

And it is a contradiction on which he founders. Iago talks of hierarchy and balance, but he sets out to support these things by breaking the very bonds of duty which keep them together. He refuses to see Othello's marriage bonds to Desdemona as proper ones. Othello talks of his 'title' as a husband, but Iago talks of the marriage as an act of piracy. (1, 2, 50) Having undermined the husband's title to his wife, he is himself destroyed by having his own title to his wife's obedience revoked by Emilia's moral outrage at what her husband has brought about: 'Tis proper I obey him, but not now.' (5, 2, 202) Ironically, Emilia's act in breaking her duty to her husband and revealing his cruelty, is an act of balance, a restoration of the kind of order Iago was obsessed by. It balances out his earlier breach of the bonds of marriage. Again, as so often in these plays, it is an act with a double dimension, a wrong that does right, a good act that is a repetition of a bad one. It is a perfect expression of the ambivalence that is everywhere in the play.

4. Time After Time

Not only does *Othello* have a double setting (Venice and Cyprus), and a double 'hero' (Iago and Othello), it also has a double sense of time. It has been pointed out since the end of the seventeenth century that there is something odd about the way that time works in the play, but not that this oddness is absolutely consistent with what Shakespeare is doing here and in all of the tragedies, making us feel that there are two over-lapping worlds present on stage at the same time.

In the first two acts of *Othello*, there is nothing strange about the way time passes. If anything, what is unusual is how few liberties are taken with time. By and large, in these two acts, the time taken to do something on stage is the time it would take in real life. The only obvious exception is that Desdemona is brought from the inn to the council chamber in the course of Othello's speech describing how he wooed her, a period of no more than two minutes. Even here, though, the fact that Othello's speech, though not particularly long, ranges over many years and many countries, successfully disguises the tele-scoping. We get used to the idea that there is no difference between the time things take on stage and the time they would take in life.

But we are given a false sense of security about time. The last three acts work in a starkly different way. At one level, the three acts seem like one continuous action, a breathless emotional and psychological wave that breaks on the shore of disaster and then recedes, leaving those who have ridden it beached and forlorn. The whole impression is one of speed, of things happening before there is time to reflect on them, Iago swept along on the perverse pleasure of his own ingenuity, Othello unable to find the calm moment of thought which might save him and Desdemona.

Working against this, though, is a different logic of time which tells us that all of these things are happening slowly, over a long period. Take the handkerchief. At one level, it is an inspired piece of improvisation by Iago, an idea seized on and carried through while his malice is in full flight. At the other level, though, Emilia tells us that 'My wayward husband hath a hundred times / Wooed me to steal it' (3, 3, 296–97), giving the impression that the whole thing has been a long-conceived plan that has taken ages to come to fruition. Or even more striking is Othello's sense of how long he has been with Desdemona in the marriage bed. In 3, 3 he talks of her 'stolen hours of lust' and of his own nights of ignorance sleeping with her and not knowing her supposed infidelities. (3, 3, 344) But only two scenes earlier he has slept with her for the first time. And the scene which separates these two is of about half a minute's duration. Scene 3, where Othello gives the impression that he has slept with Desdemona many times is effectively continuous with Scene 1 where he sleeps with her first: the action of one is continued directly in the other.

And this sense of there being two different time schemes at work becomes, if anything, stronger. In 4, 2, Othello and Emilia discuss Desdemona's behaviour with words like 'ever' and 'never', giving the impression that Othello and Desdemona have been married a long time. Othello talks of his wife having committed 'the act of shame / A thousand times' (5, 2, 218–19) which is some going if they have really only been together for one night. Similarly Bianca attacks Cassio for having been 'a week away' from her, even though, by the other time scheme they have only been together for a day or two. And, during the continuous action between the beginning of Act 3 and the end of the play, action which by one time scheme takes place between one night and the next, the Turkish threat to Cyprus disappears and peace breaks out, the Venetian senate is informed of what's going on, and decides to replace Othello with Cassio, and Lodovico has time to arrive in Cyprus from Venice with the news.

In this brilliant division of time into two different and at times competing logics, Shakespeare dramatizes the core of the play. There is a normal time in which the rest of the world and events unfold themselves in the usual way. But there is also the time of Iago and Othello. Both are out of synch with the times, Iago unable to reconcile himself to the new order, Othello ahead of the times as a man who has power but no status. This sense of the two men being out of their time becomes literal. We feel it and experience it as we watch the play, their fast, passionate time at odds with the normal unfolding of history.

This bold division of time is possible because *Othello* is a play in which things in general are refusing to stand still, in which hitherto fixed things are turning into their opposites. Most obviously, black and white, the clearest of distinctions, are melting together, both in the marriage of Othello and Desdemona and in the surrounding imagery of darkness and light. Othello himself as someone who is deeply ambiguous in his meaning for others is superbly dramatized in the opening scenes, where one group is seeking to apprehend him as a criminal and the other is seeking to appoint him as defender of the state. He is such a slippery presence, so apt to change his shape in the sight of others, that he is accused of being a magician.

Here again, Iago and Othello are alike. Othello is accused of being a magician and casting spells, but it is Iago who, in his speech, transforms people into animals and, in his plottings, transforms innocent things into 'evidence' of unfaithfulness. As Iago and Othello melt into each other, Othello starts to use Iago's language of transformation. Iago's 'I would change my humanity with a baboon' (1, 3, 315) is almost repeated in Othello's later 'Exchange me for a goat'. (3, 3, 184) And Othello becomes the magician he has been painted as. In his obsessive insistence on the significance of the handkerchief, he makes it into a magical object: 'There's magic in the web of it.' (3, 4, 69) So, while *Othello* doesn't have the ghosts and witches of *Hamlet* or *Macbeth*, it does have a sense of the magical and the ritual, of the slipperiness of things being dramatized and contained.

In this, as in so much else, what happens in the play is caught in the middle between an old way of thinking and a new one. The old way of thinking claimed that the whole cosmos was one organic unity and that therefore every part bore a sympathetic relationship to every other. The position of a star could tell you how a man on earth might behave. The look of a man's face could tell you what his mind, his soul, his inner being, were like. But Desdemona breaks with this world-view.

Instead of taking Othello's face, regarded as inferior and ugly by her society, as proof of his inner worth, she chooses to look beyond the external and to see Othello's 'visage in his mind'. (1, 3, 252) This should be enough for happiness and it would be if those around her were of like mind, if the new world to which her decision belongs had already fully arrived. But it hasn't. It hasn't arrived for Othello and it hasn't arrived for Iago.

It is precisely this relationship between outward appearances and inner worth that Iago and Othello confuse. They are neither one thing nor the other. If Othello were fully of the old way of thinking, he would stay within his 'clime, complexion, and degree'. If he were of the new way of thinking, he would adopt the scientific means of looking at things, which is to move from the external to the internal, from outward evidence to inner conviction about what the evidence means. But he does neither of these things. He breaks with the old way by shifting out of his 'proper' position, but he doesn't adopt the new way. Instead of moving from external evidence to internal conviction, he moves from his inner conviction, his conviction that Desdemona must be unfaithful, to the 'evidence', the handkerchief and Desdemona's pleading for Cassio. He moves from conviction to evidence and not, as a new humanist would do, the other way round.

The tragic irony here is that all Othello is doing is continuing the good, humane leap of faith that Desdemona has made in choosing him for her husband. She has fallen in love with him because she believes that outward evidence can be over-ridden by human emotions. And in suspecting her, Othello does the same thing, reading the evidence according to his emotions, allowing the inner feeling to override the outward appearance. This is much more than jealousy, this is a tragic turning of things into their opposites. Her good, human gesture turns into his evil, inhuman action. Her generosity becomes his narrowness. Her act of love becomes his act of self-loathing. Her sympathy becomes his violence. The refusal of things to stay fixed, the ability of things to suddenly change their natures, is what dooms them both.

And the same contradiction bedevils Iago. He at once believes that things should stay the same, that the old gradation should stay in force, and that he can transform everything, people into animals, innocence into corruption. He believes that Othello's outward appearance, his black skin, is sufficient reason to hate and fear him, but in his mind he keeps changing that appearance, imagining Othello not merely as not a black man but as not a man at all. Believing that outward appearances are everything and that they can be manipulated at will, he is undone by the fact that his wife Emilia belies her outward appearance of cynicism and emerges as being ready to die for truth and goodness. Because neither is at one with the outside world, Othello and Iago cannot get this business of inside and outside right. It is a failure that dooms them both.

4

King Lear: Zero Hour

1. Messiahs and Madmen

The world, learned men tended to agree, was old, in its dotage, on the way out. Things were changing so fast, so many unprecedented things were happening, that the end of the world might well be at hand. There was widespread speculation about its timing: in 1589, shortly after Shakespeare came to London, the courtier Anthony Marten testified to 'the number of prophets that God doth daily send to admonish all people of the latter [i.e. last] day, and to give them warning to be in a readiness'. The historian Keith Thomas has remarked on the fact that 'The reign of Elizabeth produced a small army of pseudo-Messiahs.'

And these Messiahs didn't just come from God – more to the point they came from the Heath of *King Lear*, from the great reservoir of the restless and the impoverished, the mad and the ecstatic, the dispossessed thrown on to the roads and into the open spaces by the enclosure of lands which denied the poor the use of their traditional commonage. An image frequently used in this era, from Thomas More's *Utopia* to anonymous ballads, is that of sheep eating people – the poor being devoured by the rich man's sheep which had taken over what once was common land. The social order of feudalism seemed to be giving way to something unnatural, something that could not portend good for the world. From the reservoir of the restless came the prophets, declaring themselves to be God's anointed, threatening doom unless the fences that had enclosed the common land were taken down, among them men like Captain Pouch, leader of the Midland Peasants' Revolt, who rose up claiming a divine mission to throw down the enclosures. Prophecy was political, subversive, dangerous. Usually, the government dismissed the prophets as 'brainsick' or 'fanatic', but when the prophets gathered followers and declared their political aims, immediate and violent action was taken.

In 1591, when Shakespeare was well established in London, William Hacket, an illiterate and bankrupt former servant, came to Cheapside, set himself up on the back of a cart and declared himself to be the Messiah, come to judge the world on God's behalf. He claimed gifts of prophecy and healing and threatened a series of plagues upon England unless immediate reformation took place. He gathered a 'great multitude of young persons and lads of the meaner sort' as his followers. He declared that the Privy Council must resign and that the Queen had forfeited her crown. He was arrested and executed.

But all through the years before and after the writing of *King Lear* there was a stream of William Hackets, of poor prophets threatening the end of the world unless the social order was changed and justice be given to the poor.

And it was not just the ragged and the homeless who pursued this vision of the world gone mad. The idea that folly ruled the world was a favourite of the new humanists. 'Folly,' says Erasmus of Rotterdam, 'creates kingdoms, and supports power, religion, government, and the courts. Indeed, what is all human life, if not the concern of Folly.' The world is gone so mad that only Folly can rule it. 'Foolery, sir,' says the clown Feste in Shakespeare's *Twelfth Night*, 'does walk about the orb like the sun. It shines everywhere.' Madness and blindness are the metaphors that best express the way the world is working: 'Tis the times' plague,' says Gloucester in *King Lear*, 'when madmen lead the blind.'

King Lear is Shakespeare's journey into this country of mad prophets, of social injustice, of a world ruled by Folly, of the world turned upside down. It has its prophets and its messiahs, its beggars and its madmen, its hints that the world may be coming to an end, its daring and startling political content. It uses the language of the prophets and the messiahs, and the images of the humanists, to say what might in one form be dismissed as 'brainsick' and in another be recognized as treason. Small wonder that none of Shakespeare's plays has been so uncomfortable for the critics, that none has been so much rewritten, cut, dismissed as unplayable and immoral. *King Lear* explodes out of all of the categories that the mainstream of Shakespeare criticism would try to impose on it. It has no moral lesson, its ending is patently not inevitable and even if Lear has a tragic flaw, his suffering is so much out of proportion to his flaw that it is patently absurd to suggest that he has merely brought it on himself.

The injustice of *King Lear* has annoyed many critics. That *Lear* is not a moral play is precisely the charge that has often been laid against it. Dr Johnson was distressed by the play's failure to balance the moral scales. 'Shakespeare has suffered the virtue of Cordelia to perish in a just cause, contrary to the natural ideas of justice, to the hope of the reader, and, what is yet more strange, to the faith of the chronicles . . . A play in which the wicked prosper and the virtuous miscarry may doubtless be good because it is a just representation of the common events of human life: but since all reasonable beings naturally love justice, I cannot easily be persuaded that the natural observation of justice make a play worse; or that, if other excellencies are equal, the audience will not always rise better pleased from the final triumph of persecuted virtue.' A. C. Bradley, the most influential of the Victorian critics, also wished for a happy ending – 'this catastrophe, unlike those of all the other mature tragedies, does not seem at all inevitable. It is not even satisfactorily motived.'

What Bradley wanted, and what audiences in the theatre got for a very long time in Nahum Tate's doctored version of the play, was a vision of domestic bliss at the end: 'peace and happiness by Cordelia's fireside'. What none of the play's critics could take to heart was the fact that *King Lear* moves beyond the idea of individual justice, of whether this or that person gets what they deserve, to the idea of social justice. Shakespeare gives us a play in which no justice is possible in the world as it is, in which there is so much injustice that the world may be about to end.

The other thing to be got out of the way in trying to understand what happens in *King Lear* is the idea that, because it makes use of a folktale and because the source for the play sets the story back in the mists of time, that we are in some kind of Druidic, primitive pre-Christian world. Shakespeare does make the odd effort at suggesting that this is pre-Christian England, particularly in his references to the Gods, but this is not a bad thing to do if you are about to write a play which has explosive things to say about power, government and social justice in a viciously repressive state where free speech is a dangerous thing.

Everything else in *King Lear* points to a sophisticated, developed, and not at all primitive, society. The whole theme of the play, about the relationship of the family to the state, presupposes the existence of a powerful state, of the state as a real factor in everybody's life, an idea that reflects the England of Elizabeth and James rather than of tribes and Druids. And the play's central idea of cruelty, the idea of being driven outdoors and exposed to the elements, is one which presupposes the normality of an indoor, relatively comfortable life. Furthermore, the imagery of the play, for all the pagan setting, is deeply biblical, drawn in particular from the Book of Revelations. The world we are in is the familiar one of the tragedies, a world where feudalism is giving way to capitalism, where different systems of values and different governing principles overlap, mingle and blur. We are not in a primitive, homogenous world, but in a sophisticated, rapidly changing one.

Nor is it right to suggest that *King Lear* ignores or is careless about morality. It is rather that it consciously and conclusively goes beyond morality. This is a function of the way it moves through the individual to the social but also of the very form of the play. One of the main reasons why *King Lear* is so devastating to see or even to read is that it lulls us from time to time into expecting it to be a moral play, into thinking that the normal rules of good overcoming evil will apply. Shakespeare, particularly in the last act of the play, goes through all the right forms of the conventional tragic ending, in which good is finally victorious, but only to mock them, only to expose their inefficiency.

Conventional complaints about the ending of the play – that there is no convincing re-assertion of the moral and social order at the end – forget that this is precisely the effect that Shakespeare structured the play in order to achieve. For the ending of the play is in a sense a second ending. We have already had a conventional, moral ending, the one provided by the single combat of Edmund and Edgar. In this fight, good beats evil, the conventional moral triumph is completed. It is an ending like the ending of any number of Shakespeare plays. Except that it is not the end, that it is not enough, that we are suddenly faced with this old man who comes back on stage, literally howling.

Edgar's killing of Edmund in 5, 3 has all the signs that it is the end of the play. Everybody is concerned to tell us that it's all over. Edmund confesses his sins and says 'Tis past, and so am I.' Edgar draws the handy moral of the story, the brothers are reconciled to each other. Edmund says 'The wheel is come full circle; I am here', which is as much to say 'the story is over now'. Albany comes in to pick up the pieces and to be the figure of some kind of order at the end. Edgar tells us about Gloucester's death: all the plot lines are being wrapped up. But then he says 'This would have seemed a period . . . but . . .' This should have been the end, but . . . It is the biggest *but* in theatrical history. Things start to go wrong with the moral ending in which good has vanquished evil. Edgar tells us about his encounter with Kent in terms which we cannot take to mean anything other than that Kent is dead. Eight lines later, Edgar tells us casually 'here comes Kent', Kent wanders in, and the conclusion refuses to conclude. The man we thought was dead is back on stage looking for Lear. We are brought back from the brink of a comfortable conclusion, forced to remember Lear and his suffering. Then, '*Enter Lear with Cordelia in his arms.*' Shakespeare, as Stephen Booth has put it 'presents the culminating events of his story after his play is over'. The story bursts out beyond the moral ending of the play, the overwhelming sense of injustice breaks through the even balancing of good and evil. And this isn't a failure of the play: it is the whole point of the play's structure.

There is no simple sense of morality – of what is virtue and what is vice – in *King Lear*. Take a very simple virtue, one on which the whole feudal society from which Shakespeare's times are only beginning to emerge is founded: loyalty. The loyalty of the servant to the master, of the serf to the lord, is a basic moral category in those times. Does *King Lear* endorse that morality or deny it? It does neither: it shows morality falling apart under the stress of the play's traumatic events and emotions. In the figure of Kent, who is loyal to his king even though treated outrageously by him, the play may seem to contain a relatively simple idea of faithful service. But it is an ideal that is utterly insufficient to the ferocious demands of the play. Goneril's loyal servant Oswald, for instance, is a moral wretch. The servant who kills Cornwall, on the other hand, breaks a lifetime's trust – we are told that he has been in Cornwall's service since he was a child – but on any human scale he is clearly a vastly better person than Oswald. The traditional morality of loyalty, of knowing one's place and keeping it, is no longer of much use.

Even the easiest of questions about what is good and what is bad turn out, in *King Lear*, to be not so easy after all. Who wins the final battle – the good side or the bad side? In other Shakespeare plays which end in battles – *Macbeth*, or *Julius Caesar*, or most of the history plays – we know the answer to that question. In *King Lear*, it is at best irrelevant, at worst confusing. Albany, the muddler who is desperately trying to keep hold on what is going on and who is therefore most like the audience, fights both for and against Lear and Cordelia. At the end of, say, *Henry V*, the English have beaten the French and it is an epoch-making triumph. At the end of *King Lear* the English have beaten the French and it is so meaningless that we hardly even notice. Good and bad, for and against, is a small matter when set against a grieving old man with his dead daughter in his arms.

2. Down to Zero

The play *King Lear* is a struggle between traditional bonds and duties and the question 'how much?' Duty and bonds are the values of a feudal society, 'how much?' is the basic question of a capitalist one. Lear breaks the bonds, bringing his kingdom and all the fixed relationships within it tumbling down with the question 'Which of you shall we say doth love us most?' (1, 1, 51) Because Lear is old, because he can seem to come from a timeless past, it is easy to forget that in his ambition to know how much, to quantify and measure even those things which cannot be measured, he is as much a new man as Hamlet or Macbeth, as much at odds with tradition as either of them. He is in love with numbers, until he comes to understand that there is only one absolute number: nothing. And that, as he learns, is the most terrifying number of all.

It is not that the play opens on a calm, ordered world, which Lear in his folly then proceeds to disrupt. On the contrary, only by an obsession with the tragic flaw, with the notion that Lear must be to blame for everything that happens, can the instability and precariousness of the world of the play even before Lear's break with Cordelia be missed. There are already hints of discord before Lear's division of the kingdom: the return of Edmund with his eye for the main chance, the favouring of Albany over Cornwall, hinting at dark rivalries already in existence, the manoeuvrings of the foreign princes for Cordelia's hand. Lear specifically says the reason for dividing up the kingdom now is 'the prevention of future strife', giving us to understand that the kingdom is already seething with a discord that only drastic action can prevent from coming to the surface. These are times of instability. And not just political instability. The ease with which, later in the play, a rich courtier like Edgar can turn himself into the lowest of the low, the mad beggar Poor Tom, makes it clear that there is also social instability, that, as in *Hamlet*, 'the toe of the peasant comes so near the heel of the courtier he galls his kibe'. Social distinctions have become slippery and unsure. The world of the play, in other words, is the world of Shakespeare's England.

The very first lines of *King Lear* are about comparatives. 'I thought the king had more affected the Duke of Albany than Cornwall.' The discussion between Kent and Gloucester is about the valuation of people – Albany as against Cornwall – in a way that measures them by the worth of their land. This is Lear's way of thinking: nothing has a value in itself, only in comparison with something else. The question that he and his courtiers ask of something is not what it's like but how much it's worth in relation to something else. Many of the characters in the opening scene are identified by what they own – their very names are the names of tracts of land: Kent, Gloucester, Albany, France, Burgundy. And Lear in turn identifies places, not with the people in them, but with their profitable produce. The first time he introduces the subject of Cordelia's marriage he proposes not to marry her to the man who is called France or the man who is called Burgundy but to the 'Vines of France and milk of Burgundy'. (1, 1, 84) These flesh and blood men disappear in the way Lear talks and are replaced by the tradeable goods that their lands produce.

For a man like this to demand a comparative valuation of love itself, as he does of his three daughters, is hardly surprising. In this, Lear far from being a man from the mists of time, is not even a feudal lord – he is an archetype of the new middle-class man. He confuses having something and being something, believing that because he has so much he must indeed be wonderful, that because his power is limitless, so too must he be infinitely loved. This conviction that you are what you have is the characteristic delusion of middle-class man, the kind that is on the rise at the time the play is written.

Goneril picks up on this way of thinking and sets out to satisfy it: her description of her love is all comparisons: more, dearer, beyond, no less than, as much as – these are the terms in which she speaks. The irony in her speech is that her love is indeed beyond all value, since it doesn't exist at all. The thing that is really beyond all comparisons is nothing, and that nothing is what will come to haunt Lear as the play goes on. In a strange way, Goneril is telling the truth, just as, in a sense, Cordelia is telling a lie. Goneril's love is as she says, 'Beyond what can be valued', while Cordelia's is not truly encompassed by the stark and flat words she uses. What Goneril claims of her own love 'I love you more than word can wield the matter' is in fact true of Cordelia.

Why does Cordelia not join in this game of puffed-up language for the sake of peace and quiet? Wouldn't it be better for her to tell a small lie for the sake of a greater truth – that she does indeed love Lear more than either of her sisters do? The obsession with the tragic flaw has even made some commentators go so far as to give one to Cordelia, to sow the seeds of her own destruction in her foolish refusal to play the game. But the fact is that Cordelia cannot join in this game of inflated language, for the very terms of that language, the whole notion of a comparison of things, is outside her way of thinking.

Cordelia's way of thinking and feeling is fundamentally feudal. She refuses Lear's attempts to get her to define her love in quantative terms because those terms are completely outside her view of the world. She rejects both absolutes and comparisons and is concerned only for what is and what should be: 'I love your Majesty / According to my bond, no more nor less.' She is not interested in quantities, in Lear's demand to know whether one thing is more than another, because in the feudal way of thinking, there are no real comparisons. The world is an enclosed order in which everything has its place, in which all, from the highest to the lowest, are part of the system of the universe, of the general scheme of things. And it is precisely on the scheme of things that Cordelia bases her answer. She says 'no more nor less' – none of this business of comparing one thing to another, things are either in their right place or they are not, my love is either as it should be between a daughter and her father and a subject and her King (for Lear, of course, is both King and father to Cordelia, and she stresses this very deliberately by calling him 'your Majesty') or it is nothing. Lear, blinded by his obsession with the quantity of things, decides that it must be nothing. And with his calculator out, as it were, he declares that 'Nothing will come of nothing.' He could not, as he will learn, be more wrong.

This clash of two different ways of thinking, one feudal and one modern, is made much more explicit in the next scene (1, 2) where we get two complete world-views, one from Gloucester and the other from Edmund, side by side. Gloucester, upset by the false evidence of Edgar's treachery planted by Edmund, gives us his version of the world in which man is governed by the state of the universe, in which human behaviour and emotion, including the love of parent and child which we have just seen disputed in the first scene, are governed by 'these late eclipses in the sun and moon'. It is a feudal view of the world taken to absurd extremes. He goes out and Edmund immediately gives us a completely different version of the way the world works. His is the world of the self-made man, in which we have no one else but ourselves to blame for our sins and no one else to thank for our good fortune. Belief in the influence of the planets on human behaviour – a basic idea in the feudal world-view – is, to him, 'an admirable evasion of whoremaster man'. 'I should have been that I am had the maidenliest star in the firmament twinkled on my bastardizing.' Edmund's statement that 'let me, if not by birth, have lands by wit . . .' is the perfect summation of the new individualism, the new determination not to be bound by the rule of custom which Edmund sees as a 'plague' (1, 2, 3) and on which Cordelia bases her whole sense of herself, as a subject, a daughter and a wife. If ever there were two opposing views of the world that are tearing the universe apart, it is in *King Lear*.

With this context created, the numbers game of the play goes on. In the hyping up of language indulged in by Goneril and Regan in the first scene, the idea of the absolute – the most you can possibly love someone – got mixed up with the idea of nothing, the ultimate absolute, the real figure of Regan and Goneril's love for Lear. Lear's belief that nothing would come of nothing is already undermined in the second scene. The letter which Edmund has forged is a nothing – a complete lie:

> *Gloucester:* What paper are you reading?
> *Edmund:* Nothing, my lord. (1, 2, 31–32)

But it is a nothing that is parallel to Regan and Goneril's fine words – an inflated piece of language that really amounts to nothing at all, and is therefore, like those words, dangerous. Grimly, if unintentionally, Gloucester utters the prophetic 'The quality of nothing hath not such need to hide itself.' (1, 2, 33) And, indeed, nothing will show itself, for that nothing will be Lear himself.

It is this imagery of nothing, this game of numbers that moves down to zero that makes sense of what can seem like the most tedious scene of the play, the whole debate about the number of knights that Lear is to have in his retinue in Act 2, scene 4. Already by the end of Act 1, the Fool has specifically identified Lear with the number nought: 'now thou art an 0 without a figure. I am better than thou art now: I am a fool, thou art nothing.' (1, 4, 174–75) Now, in 2, 4 this whittling down of Lear to nothing is acted out before us. Lear is still insisting on measuring love by numbers ('Thy fifty yet doth double five and twenty / And thou art twice her love.') but

Goneril and Regan again seize on his way of thinking as they did in the first scene, this time using it to bait him rather than to flatter him. They systematically reduce the numbers that he is worth from 100 to 50 to 25 to 10 to 5 to 1 to 0, the '0 without a figure' that the Fool told Lear he had become and to which he is now reduced before our eyes. Now, the only numbers that Lear has to play with are not the numbers of power and possession but the numbers of sorrow: 'this heart / Shall break into a hundred thousand flaws / Or ere I'll weep.' Lear is still inflating numbers but now in pain instead of pomp: a heart broken into a hundred thousand pieces is no heart at all. In his hurt he has begun to see himself as nothing.

As the play goes on, the whole idea of numbers becomes a mad joke. Lear tells us his age is 'Fourscore and upward / Not an hour more or less', (4, 6, 55–56) a phrase that, in its mock precision, seems to continue his obsession with quantities, but now without meaning. The treachery of numbers is now out in the open: the phrase seems to tell us precisely a basic fact about Lear but all it really does is to mock the belief that numbers can really tell us anything worth knowing, the very belief in quantity with which Lear opened the whole story.

In the second half of the play, indeed, the whole notion of comparing one thing with another, of more and less, has turned from power to pain. Now the things to be measured against each other are not love or pieces of land or produce, but anguish and affliction. The world is turned upside down, so that the quantifiers have nothing to quantify but desolation. At the start of Act 3, scene 4, Lear is measuring afflictions against each other as he formerly measured the love of his daughters: 'where the greater malady is fix'd / The lesser is scarce felt.' (8–9) Shortly afterwards, at the start of Act 4, Edgar is trying to measure woes, to define the worst that things can get. And again, the action of the play mocks this urge to quantify. Trying to cheer himself up, he says that he has reached the 'worst' and that things can only get better: 'The worst returns to laughter'. (4, 1, 6) Immediately, Shakespeare sends on Edgar's father Gloucester, blinded and despairing. Edgar is forced to cry:

> O gods! Who is't can say 'I am the worst'?
> I am worse that e'er I was . . .
> And worse I may be yet.

Lear thought that power was limitless. What he and Edgar learn is that the only thing that is limitless is suffering. In it, as Cordelia said of her love at the beginning, there is no more nor less. Like Macbeth who murdered sleep and will sleep no more, Lear has broken the limits of things and will know no more limits to what can happen to him.

3. Beyond The Limits

In the battle between order and power, between feudal system and individual will, that is raging through *King Lear*, basic categories and fundamental oppositions fall apart. Lear breaks the bond of family – 'Here I disclaim all my paternal care' – and in doing so he unleashes a breakdown in the basic categories of father and daughter, parent and child, man and woman. In the imagery of the play, these fundamental notions of human identity, the roles in which the personal and the social should come together in harmony, fall apart.

The whole notion of fatherhood, in which Lear places such store, is among the first of the fixed ideas of family to go. Edmund challenges the idea that having a legitimate, socially endorsed father is a necessary part of being a proper human being ('Now, gods, stand up for bastards.' 1, 2, 22) and Lear is forced himself to recognise that legitimate fatherhood is of no use in determining the worth of your children, for Regan and Goneril were 'Got 'tween the lawful sheets.' (4, 5, 115) It is not just the family, but the whole idea of heredity, the belief that children have anything but an accidental relationship to their parents, that is falling apart.

The whole meaning of words like 'daughter', 'mother', 'husband', and 'wife' comes into question, as do the categories of father and child. In the letter that Edmund forges in 1, 2, Edgar supposedly talks of reversing the roles of father and son, 'the father should be as the ward to the son, and the son manage his revenue.' (75) The Fool tells Lear 'thou hads't made thy daughters thy mothers' (1, 4, 153) and pictures the ancient Lear as a little boy bending down to be caned by his mother/daughters. Goneril decides to become her husband and to make him into a woman ('I must change arms at home, and give the distaff / Into my husband's hands' 4, 2, 17 – 'distaff' being the symbol of womanhood.) When Goneril says 'My fool usurps my body' (4, 2, 28) she means that Albany is not a fit husband for her, and that Edmund is more worthy of her, but the way she says it also implies, coming so soon after her image of making Albany a woman, that that image is continuing and that she is picturing Albany as herself and herself as Albany.

And indeed this is in keeping with the way we experience the play: at the start it is Albany whom we suspect of jealousy and greed (the opening line has him contending with Cornwall for the king's favour) and Goneril who is protesting her love for Lear. As the play goes on they change places: she seeking dominance and power, he protesting his sympathy for Lear. This is why Albany is such a deliberately weak image of the restoration of order at the end: he is a different man, a half-formed character whom Shakespeare has gone to great lengths to make ambivalent, confused, an image of the way we ourselves as an audience must feel at the end. This imagery of sexual confusion in which Goneril in particular refuses to remain fixed in her womanhood is completed by what Lear says when he sees Gloucester in Act 4, scene 6: 'Ha! Goneril with a white beard!' In the upside-down world into which we have been thrown, there is a crazy logic to this madness: Goneril has been 'becoming' her men, Edmund is now her lover and Edmund is now the Earl of Gloucester, having 'become' his father by taking his title. As the people around him understand, Lear is mad but there is a logic running through his madness. 'O, matter and impertinency mix'd!' says Edgar of Lear's language. 'Reason in madness!' (4, 6, 170)

There is, though, another more enigmatic but ultimately more powerful sexual confusion that runs through the play. It is in the strange way that the Fool and Cordelia, a man and a woman, act largely as one character in the play. It is not just that the two characters are never on stage at the same time – that when Cordelia leaves the Fool appears, and when the Fool disappears, Cordelia is back – though that is an important part of the way we are made to feel this merging of the two characters. It is also that the two play precisely the same role in relation to Lear – that of telling him the uncomfortable truth. And the confusion, of course, reaches its height in Lear's final speech, where, with Cordelia in his arms, he says 'And my poor fool is hang'd.' (5, 3, 281) 'Fool' itself is one of the most slippery words in the play, having, at times, completely contradictory meanings. It is, for instance, used as both the opposite of 'knave' ('The fool no knave', 2, 2, 225) and as another word for 'knave' ('Poor fool and knave', 3, 2, 72), and this disturbing doubleness of the word becomes complete when, at the most emotionally charged moment of the play, we are deliberately made unsure as to whether 'fool' refers to the Fool or, used in the Elizabethan sense of an innocent creature or child, to Cordelia, Lear's innocent child. Given the very deliberate way in which Shakespeare has made the word unstable throughout the play, we have to accept that it refers to both at the same time, that Fool and Cordelia have become one in Lear's mind, as, in a sense, they have in the mind of the audience. When you remember that in Shakespeare's theatre, the same actor would almost certainly have played the Fool and Cordelia (women characters were played by boys, making the sexual confusion both starker and funnier, another theatrical in-joke that reminds us that we are watching a play and not 'reality') then the point of the confusion becomes more obvious.

Shakespeare is giving us a world in which the borders of identity, including sexual identity, are collapsing under the strain of traumatic social change.

The chant of the witches in *Macbeth* – 'Double, double' – could also be a slogan for *King Lear* as in the play it's not just sexual identity that becomes double, but everything else. Because things refuse to hold their borders, we get two of everything. Most obviously, there are two evil sisters (Goneril and Regan), two sons of Gloucester (Edmund and Edgar), two Earls of Gloucester (Gloucester himself and Edmund), two suitors for Cordelia's hand (France and Burgundy), two sons-in-law (Albany and Cornwall). Most of the characters exist in our minds as one half of a gang of two.

And the most memorable and shocking action that we see on stage – the blinding of Gloucester – is deliberately double. It is double, indeed, in two ways. First we are given it as an idea from Gloucester himself, but applied to someone else, to Lear: 'I would not see thy cruel nails / Pluck out his poor old eyes.' (4, 1, 54–55) Then it is taken up by Cornwall and turned back on Gloucester himself. And what makes the act particularly shocking is that we are forced to watch it, as it were, twice. Shakespeare could have had Gloucester blinded in a single action, but instead he deliberately places a dramatic and intense piece of action – the killing of Cornwall by the servant – between the plucking out of one eye and another. The double nature of the event is stressed by Regan: 'One side will mock another; th' other too.' And when the event is reported to Albany soon afterwards, he is not told simply that Gloucester's eyes have been put out. It is the doubleness of

113

what has happened that is stressed. The messenger tells him that Cornwall has been killed 'going to put out the other eye of Gloucester.' (4, 2, 38–39) Nobody talks about the first eye, only the second; only, as it were, the double:

> *Albany:* Lost he his other eye?
> *Messenger:* Both, both, my lord. (48–49)

When the world has become like this – two worlds at the same time – then the whole idea of cause and effect breaks down. It is only if you have one world, one set of rules that don't change, that a particular cause can have a predictable effect. This doesn't happen in *King Lear*. Lear sets out to prevent future strife and unleashes strife by doing so. And even before Lear announces this intention to us, Shakespeare has placed an ominous image of cause and effect breaking down. The cause of Edmund, the 'good sport' that Gloucester had at his making, is completely out of synch with the effect that he will have for Gloucester – blindness and death.

Cause and effect is itself the subject of Edmund's speech on astrology, which rejects Gloucester's feudal contention that what happens in the world can be traced back to a fundamental cause in the workings of the universe. Edmund sees himself as an uncaused man, literally a rebel without a cause: 'Fut, I should have been that I am, had the maidenliest star in the firmament twinkled on my bastardizing.' (1, 2, 128) And he specifically links this rejection of the idea of cause and effect with the rise of the new man, of which he is the great example. His whole rebellion is a rebellion against the notion that things that have happened in the past – the circumstances of your birth or conception – should have an effect on the present. With this rebellion in progress, in the play and in Shakespeare's world, the consequences of actions cannot be foreseen, causes cannot be traced, the future cannot be controlled or predicted. Lear can no more prevent future strife than he can out-roar the wind.

This is why so much of what happens at the end of the play is gratuitous. A gratuitous action is one which has no clear cause, which is not obviously the effect of something that has been done in the past. The complaint that has been made about the gratuitousness of, say, Cordelia's death, misses the point that what Shakespeare is showing us is precisely the breakdown of the idea of cause and effect. Cordelia's death is shattering precisely because it undermines our faith in the idea that there is a logical connection between the thing that happens and the thing that has caused it. And the circumstances of that death are constructed so as to stress this. The one successful physical act that Lear performs in the whole play – the killing of the man who is hanging Cordelia – a heroic effort of will for a maddened old man, is completely useless because it does not achieve its purpose: the saving of Cordelia. Actions, even the one truly decisive action that Lear takes in the whole play, cannot have their desired effects.

What we have, therefore, is a failure of things to add up or to keep to their places. Characters don't stay as they are but seem to take on each other's roles. Who, for instance, is the Fool? At the start, we know that he can say what he says because his role is well-defined, because he is licensed to say what no one else can. But as the play goes on, it seems as if everyone is auditioning for his part. Not only does Cordelia shadow the Fool, becoming, in the end, virtually indistinguishable from him, but Lear, Kent and Edgar all seem to fancy themselves as Fools. In Act 1, scene 5, Lear engages in such adept banter with the Fool that the Fool tells him: 'Thou wouldst make a good fool.' Kent, in disguise, presents himself in his interview for a job as Lear's servant as if he were a professional jester:

> *Lear:* What art thou?
> *Kent:* A very honest-hearted fellow and as poor as the King.
> *Lear:* If thou be'st as poor for a subject as he's for a king, thou art poor enough . . . (1, 4, 18–22)

If we didn't know that this was Kent speaking, we would swear it was the Fool, and Lear talks to him exactly as he talks to the Fool. There is an appropriateness about this usurpation of the Fool's privileges by Kent, for Kent is where he is precisely for having usurped the Fool's role of telling the truth to Lear. Similarly, Edgar, in his disguise as Poor Tom, exchanges banter with Lear, Kent and Gloucester in a style that echoes that of the Fool, and takes over the Fool's habit of breaking out in snatches of obscure song. With these disguised men trying to become the Fool, it is not hard to think of the Fool himself as a kind of disguised Cordelia.

It is hardly surprising that the imagery of the play has so much to do with limits and borders breaking down, with people even turning into animals. It is as a force which breaks down

116

natural borders and limits that Albany sees his wife Goneril. Her nature 'cannot be bordered certain in itself' (scene 16, line 33, in the first quarto version of the play); she will 'sliver and disbranch from her material sap.' (line 34) And in that breaking down, the borders between the human and the animal world disappear, in such a way as to reinforce the disappearance of barriers between the individual personalities of the play. Goneril and Regan are compared to animals – snakes, boars, wolves, dogs, tigers – and even more nightmarishly to monsters that are half-human and half-animal. A servant in Act 3, scene 7 tells us that 'Women will all turn monsters.' Albany tells Goneril to 'Be-monster not thy features.' (scene 16, line 63) Lear pictures his daughters as half-woman, half-horse: 'Down from the waist they are centaurs / Though women all above'. (4, 5, 121–22) In a world where people have become half animal, Lear pictures Cordelia as dying because she is all human and not animal:

> Why should a dog, a horse, a rat have life,
> And thou no breath at all? (5, 3, 282–83)

And in the imagery of the play, it is not just individual people who turn animal, but the whole world of power and politics. Take the image of people as dogs. The way Lear's logic works, he associates it first with Goneril and Regan, then with himself, and then with the whole tyrannical system of government with which they are involved. He imagines his daughters as dogs ('see, they bark at me', 3, 6, 21), then himself as dog – 'They flattered me like a dog' (4, 5, 96) – and then of political power itself as dog-like:

Lear: Thou has't seen a farmer's dog bark at a beggar?
Gloucester: Ay, sir.
Lear: And the creature run from the cur? There thou
    mightst behold the great image of authority: a dog's
    obeyed in office. (4, 5, 150–)

In this nightmarish crossing of the borders between the human and the animal and between one person and another, Lear comes to see his daughters in himself and therefore to see his own kingly power as corrupted and unjust. It is striking that some of the animal images which are applied to Regan and Goneril are also applied to Lear by himself and others. The image of his daughters as wolves reminds us that he sees himself as 'comrade with the wolf and owl' and that Gloucester also compares him with a wolf (3, 7, 61). And if Lear compares Goneril to a sea-monster, it is worth remembering that he has already seen himself as a dragon ('Come not between the dragon and his wrath', 1, 1, 122) which is not much different. It is because Lear comes to sense the similarities between himself and his cruel daughters – their shared arrogance of power – that he comes to see power itself, in the form of remote political authority, as nothing more than a dog barking at a beggar.

4. Out in the Wild

King Lear has no ghosts or witches, not because it is outside of the ritual world of *Hamlet* and *Macbeth* but because it is so much inside that world that it doesn't need ghosts and witches as emblems of it. The world of *King Lear*, where blindness is sight and folly is wisdom, is also a world where life and death are not well separated from each other, where the notion of spirits and devils and the living dead is so centrally a part of life, that it doesn't need to be made explicit. Why have witches, when Regan and Goneril, ordinary human beings, can be repeatedly imagined as devils and monsters, can, in the imagery, change their shape into that of various animals more easily than any witch. Why have ghosts when a character like Kent whom one minute we think is dead can suddenly reappear from the 'dead' without so much as a look of surprise flickering across the faces of the others? Characters move in and out of the play, disappear and reappear, change their shape and adopt disguises, with such fluidity that real people can easily be mistaken for spirits. The Fool when he first sees Poor Tom, takes him for a 'spirit' and cries for help. (3, 4, 38) Lear, on being united with Cordelia, believes them both to be dead already. Of himself he says 'You do me wrong to take me out o' th' grave.' (4, 7, 38) Of her, he says, like the Fool seeing Poor Tom, 'You are a spirit, I know. Where did you die?' *King Lear* is at least as much concerned with finding a ritual for its times as any of the other tragedies are.

The play in fact begins with an aborted ritual, and it is the failure of that ritual that pitches the characters out into a much more difficult and dangerous kind of ritual altogether. The whole opening scene of the division of the kingdom is clearly conceived by Lear as the ritual conclusion to business already completed. It is a formal ceremonial, as Lear stresses by asking his daughters to speak in the order of their birth. It is also a ritual in another sense: in the medieval world the end of one's life, the passage from this world into the next, is thought of as a ritual. Lear sees the division of the kingdom as a ceremony marking the beginning of his death: 'Conferring them on younger strengths, while we / Unburdened crawl toward death.' (1, 1, 40–41). But both of these rituals are disrupted by Cordelia's refusal to play her allotted part. The division of the kingdom cannot go ahead as planned and Lear cannot die, but must embark on a series of events that will 'upon the rack of this tough world / Stretch him out longer.' (5, 3, 290–91)

Because these formal ceremonials fall apart, Lear is sent out into the vastly wilder ritual of the heath. The common ritual in which men leave their society and wander in the wilderness in the guise of madmen in order to gain some insight has to be enacted. What makes this ritual deeply political and subversive in *King Lear* is that in it Shakespeare takes us into the realms of the outcast prophets and malcontents that were a real feature of his own society. The language of the heath is the language of the prophets and the preachers who could say what they said only by being seen as 'brainsick', the language of their railing against the corruption of authority and the terrible nature of social injustice.

It is no accident that in *King Lear* so many of the characters want to be the Fool, want his licence to speak what is otherwise doomed to remain unspoken. A major concern of the play as a whole is the freedom to speak that the guise of foolery or madness allows. In the heath scene, under the guise of mad, apparently disordered language, Shakespeare himself takes that freedom. And, as Edgar says of Lear's speech, there is reason in madness.

What links the two rituals – the failed one of the division of the kingdom and the wild one on the heath – is the imagery of the last judgement and the Book of Revelations, the part of the Bible from which the 'mad' preachers drew their inspiration. The idea of judgement and the idea of the apocalypse are strongly linked in popular images from the thirteenth century onwards. And the notion of judgement is linked, too, to the idea of political power. Public power was measured by the extent of the area over which one exercised judgement. Lear, in the opening scene, is acting like God on the Last Day, exercising his judgement over the world as he knows it.

By the third act, that implicit imagery has come back on Lear with a vengeance, for now he pictures the storm on the heath as the last judgement itself, and he sees it the way the mad preachers see it, as the great event that brings all hidden iniquities to light and levels all inequalities:

> Let the great gods,
> That keep this dreadful pother o'er our heads,
> Find out their enemies now. Tremble, thou wretch,
> That hast within thee undivulged crimes
> Unwhipp'd of justice . . . (3, 2, 49–53)

Later, Lear pictures himself as a preacher ('I will preach to thee', 4, 5, 176) but the Fool and Edgar as Poor Tom also take on this character of the outcast revolutionary preacher. The Fool delivers his mocking prophecy (3, 2, 79–) which is very black humour indeed, for the prophecy is a description of things as they already are and his 'Then shall the realm of Albion / Come to great confusion' is, if anything, an understatement of the situation in which he and Lear find themselves. The Fool uses prophecy exactly as the mad revolutionaries use it: not to tell the future, but to tell the present.

Edgar is even more an image of the preachers of the roads, for, like them, he takes on the role of a kind of Christ. Like Christ he is a young man who goes into the wilderness, 'cures' a blind man (his father Gloucester), is, as Poor Tom, tempted by devils ('The prince of darkness is a gentleman; Modo he's called, and Mahu', 3, 4, 134–35) and then disappears. At the third blast of the trumpet ('Enter Edgar, armed, at the third sound, a trumpet before him') he reveals his true self and emerges triumphant.

All of this builds towards the imagery of the end of the world with which the play culminates. In this terrible vision, the play ends as it began, with a foolish king trying to divide the rule of his country into three. Albany asks Kent and Edgar to take over the kingdom between them (though whether in cooperation with himself or not, is far from clear): 'Friends of my soul, you twain / Rule in this realm . . .' But the sense of the end of things is so strong that both seem to refuse, seeing no future in which they might rule. Kent believes that he himself is to die shortly; Edgar seems to believe that they are all to die in the near future: 'We that are young / Shall never see so much nor live so long.'

This evocation of the end of the world has both a dramatic logic and a political one. The dramatic logic is simply that more has been lost in the play than we can ever imagine being replaced. It is not just that the older generation of Lear and Gloucester has been decimated, but that the younger generation, to whom the future should be entrusted, has suffered even worse: Cordelia, Regan, Goneril, Cornwall, and Edmund are all dead. It is not just the good with whom we sympathized, but also the evil, whose youthful energy was a highly attractive contrast to the decrepit, clapped-out atmosphere of old age, who will be missed by the audience. The political logic is that, since all the truth about the society and its injustice and hypocrisy has come tumbling out on the heath, this world cannot go on, cannot continue as if nothing had happened. The last thing we hear in the play is Edgar's linking of his sense that the world may be ending with his order to 'Speak what we feel, not what we ought to say.' For on the heath, Shakespeare has allowed things to be said which ought not to be said.

5. Nothing Comes from Nothing

The centre of *King Lear*, both literally and thematically, is the ferocious assault on authority and injustice that makes up the third and fourth acts of the play. Here, the play moves outdoors, out into the territory of the dispossessed, the brainsick preachers, the 'great multitude of young persons and lads of the meaner sort'. We are with Lear on the heath, with Gloucester and Edgar on the road to Dover, and the roads and heaths are themselves a powerful political symbol, for they are

123

the England of the poor, of those who have been thrown off their common lands by enclosures. These two acts begin with Kent's question 'Who's there, besides foul weather?' and proceed to show us just who is there, to change the perspective of aristocrats like Lear, Kent and Gloucester so that they can see the people over whom they had ruled. It is a process that Shakespeare leads us through twice over, once in the apparent madness of the heath, but then again, through the sane Edgar's manipulation of his blind father. And in both cases, this discovery of the common people is strongly linked to the theme of 'nothing' that runs through the play. We have seen Lear being whittled down to nothing in the argument with his daughters, and Gloucester being deprived, not only of his sight, but also of his very name, which is given to Edmund. And we have seen this in the light of Lear's apparently logical claim that nothing comes from nothing, that nothing itself is sheer emptiness. But in the society of the play there is a nothing that is also something: the common people who are as nothing in the world of lords and rulers but who, as will be discovered, are the common humanity to which Lear and Gloucester must belong if they are to remain human. Lear and Gloucester having broken their own families, must find for themselves the family of mankind. When Lear divided up his kingdom at the start of the play, it didn't even occur to him that there were people in it: he listed the forests, the fields, the rivers, the meadows, but not the human occupants whom he was leaving to the tender mercies of Regan and Goneril. Now, those ordinary people start to become a presence in the drama as the nothing from which any hope that there is in the play must spring. Shakespeare, astonishingly, sets out to make us see this nothing on the stage.

As we move into Act 3, the poor are literally absent. The hovel on the heath is empty, uninhabited except for Edgar as Poor Tom. And Poor Tom is a literal nothing – a man who doesn't exist, someone whom Edgar is only pretending to be. But that nothing is gradually filled as Edgar becomes, in turn, every type of poor person there is in England: a madman, a beggar, a servant ('A serving man, proud in heart and mind', 3, 4, 79), and, later (in 4, 6) a peasant speaking in a thick country accent. Through Poor Tom, and through his discovery of his own human sympathy for the Fool's suffering, Lear discovers the injustice that he himself has been careless of:

> Poor naked wretches, wheresoe'er you are,
> That bide the pelting of this pitiless storm,
> How shall your houseless heads and unfed sides,
> Your loop'd and window'd raggedness, defend you
> From seasons such as these? O', I have ta'en
> Too little care of this! Take physic, pomp;
> Expose thyself to feel what wretches feel,
> That thou may'st shake the superflux to them,
> And show the heavens more just. (3, 4, 28–)

Lear sees the shared humanity of himself and Poor Tom: both are 'unaccommodated man . . . a poor, bare, forked animal'.

Two scenes later, we see the viciousness of those in power with the blinding of Gloucester, and then something that is extraordinary in high Shakespearian tragedy: the poor, the servants, taking on a major role in the play, becoming visible and having a substantial effect on the plot. Three things happen one after the other: first, a servant kills an aristocrat, Cornwall. Then the ending of one of the most dramatic scenes in all of Shakespeare is left to two servants, who are allowed to talk to each other and not their masters. And then, almost at the start of the next act, Act 4, we have an old tenant in charge of his master, leading him along, and defying the fearful authority of Regan and Cornwall in doing so. The common people have come, for a time at least, to occupy the stage.

Lear's discovery of the common humanity which he shared with Poor Tom is repeated almost exactly by Gloucester, who in his misery, is driven to share his money with Poor Tom, echoing almost exactly Lear's speech on the need to 'shake the superflux' to the poor (i.e. give the excess wealth of the rich to the poor):

> Let the superfluous and lust-dieted man
> That slaves your ordinance, that will not see
> Because he does not feel, feel your power quickly;
> So distribution should undo excess,
> And each man have enough. (4, 1, 61–)

Act 4, scene 6 is both an extraordinary piece of theatre, and also, if it is not understood in this political context, the most baffling part of the play. Why does Edgar torment his already tortured father with the whole charade about the cliff top, pretending that he is on 'the extreme verge' of the cliff when he is not? In the first place, it is an image of going beyond the limit, literally past the edge, that, unlike all other images of the same kind in the play, is positive. Instead of being merely terrifying, Gloucester gains something from it. In the second place, it is an image of the change of perspective that the powerful must undergo if they are to see properly. Just as Lear, from his high social position, can see nothing of the people he rules, so Edgar summons up for his father an image of how the world looks from his lofty position:

> Half-way down
> Hangs one that gathers samphire – dreadful trade!
> Methinks he seems no bigger than his head.
> The fishermen that walk upon the beach
> Appear like mice . . . (4, 5, 16–)

It is only from the heights of power and prestige that a fisherman or a herb-gatherer (samphire is a herb that grows on cliffs) can look like a mouse. It is only from such heights that a man like Lear or Gloucester can overlook the human suffering around him, can 'not see because he does not feel'. Having made the descent, having put his feet on the ground that the common people walk on, Gloucester can, as he says to Lear shortly afterwards 'see . . . feelingly'. (4, 5, 145).

Even more remarkably, though, what the episode does is to make 'nothing' into a real presence on the stage. The cliff that Gloucester jumps from does not exist – it is a nothing. Yet, through the eyes of a blind man, we come to see this nothing, come to feel its presence as part of the action. Nothing becomes something and by facing it and passing through it, something can be gained from all the torment, some sense of belonging to the wider family of humanity.

It is directly after this changing of Gloucester's perspective on the world that we get the play's most savagely political speech from Lear. Lear's earlier speech about the 'poor naked wretches' and Gloucester's giving away of his money could be taken as examples of the feudal concern for a balance within society, though the passionate sense of equality that runs through them suggests that they are more than that. Lear's speech at 4, 6, 150, though, goes well beyond any such piety to attack the stupidity of authority and the hypocrisy of justice. In the cliff-top scene we have seen Edgar turn from one person at the top of the cliff to another at the bottom, and Lear now makes this switching from the top of the heap to the bottom fiercely political. He makes the sinner and the judge, the cheater and the cheated, the depraved and the supposedly upright, change places, so that those who were on top are now on the bottom. 'See how yond justice rails upon yond simple thief. Hark in thine ear: change places, and, handy-dandy, which is the justice, which is the thief?' (4, 6, 153–)

Lear takes what could be the mystical imagery of the cliff-top scene and makes it into scathing political satire. Gloucester, who has 'seen' what he could not see – the cliff – is told by Lear to:

Get thee glass eyes,
And, like a scurvy politician, seem
To see the things thou dost not. (4, 5, 166–68)

What happens to both Lear and Gloucester in this remarkable scene is that they move finally beyond the world of comparisons, of questions like 'how much?' They come down to the brute fact of their existence, to the fact that they *are* and that comparing either to anything else is meaningless. Seeing his blind father meet with the mad Lear, Edgar is struck by precisely this fact, by the way that their existence could not be expressed in any other terms than the simple fact that it *is*:

> I would not take this from report; it *is*,
> And my heart breaks at it. (4, 5, 137–38, my italics)

This, indeed, is something – a social vision – come from nothing. And this, too, is the meaning of Cordelia for Lear. Her words 'Nothing my lord' in the first scene of the play made her nothing in Lear's eyes, but it is precisely as nothing, as an absence, that she is most powerful in the play. Lear has thought of her as a valuable piece of property, had seen her in monetary terms ('When she was dear to us, we did hold her so; / But now her price is fallen . . .'). When she is lost to him, as Edgar was lost to Gloucester, she becomes a human presence in his mind. When he stops thinking in terms of money and quantity and recognizes that wealth and power have no real meaning, then he is able to find Cordelia again. Immediately after the scene in which Lear reveals, as much for himself as for his listeners, the true nature of authority, he does indeed find Cordelia again. But Cordelia has been so powerful an absence that she never really inhabits the stage a second time. Having been the great exemplar of the power of nothing, she cannot really become something again.

Cordelia's death is gratuitous but it is also dramatically necessary, for in the upside-down world of the last part of the play, it is when she is alive and on stage that she is at her weakest as a presence. Alive, she is a pale and colourless figure. She appears so fleetingly and with so little sense of personality that it is not surprising that Lear takes her at first for a spirit. Dead, she becomes a potent figure again, with the power to move both Lear and the audience to unbearable emotions. As a dead nothing again, she is able to make something come of her nothingness: grief, anger, contempt for the power of the mighty, and, above all, a sense of our common humanity. After the image of social injustice that we have seen and experienced in the third and fourth acts of the play, it is foolish to ask that the play end justly. The whole thrust of the play has been to show us an unjust world in which each human being is connected to all humanity. Within such a world, individual justice, justice for Lear and Cordelia, could not be possible. Both Lear and Gloucester have spoken about excess and superfluity, and the whole point of the end of the play is that it is excessive and superfluous, that it comes after what we are made to feel should be the end of the play – the triumph of Edgar over Edmund. One excess, the excessive wealth of the rich and powerful, is linked to the other – the excessive suffering of Lear and Cordelia. So long as there is no justice in humanity, there can be no justice for individual humans. Shakespeare makes us feel superfluousness, excess, as something immensely painful. If there is a hope in *King Lear* it is not that the world might suddenly prove to be just after all, but that, before it is too late, the world might be changed.

5

Macbeth: Back to the Future

1. Why Witches?

The witches in *Macbeth* are an embarrassment. Like refugees from an over-enthusiastic Halloween party they wander into this otherwise serious play about power and death and the evils of being too ambitious. They pull ugly faces and mutter mumbo-jumbo about toads and livers. It's not even as if they can be just cut out: not only does the play not make sense without them but, in a way, they are more real than anyone else on stage. We see them first, they define the reality that we are to see as the play goes on. Not only that, but they know more about what's really going on than anyone else. Actually, and unforgivably, they are closer to the audience's point of view than anyone else in the play: they share their confidences with us, let us know about the little game they are playing with Macbeth, function as a kind of audience themselves, maintaining their distance from the action but egging it on to its conclusion.

The best thing to do is to explain them away. They are Shakespeare's way of flattering the new King James, who was fascinated by witches. They are the remnants of a culture that we can no longer understand – terrifying then, laughable now. But the witches in *Macbeth* are not much like the witches that James was interested in: they slip through definitions rather than being theologically and socially defined as James would have had it. And far from being terrifyingly exotic in the world of *Macbeth*, they are merely examples of the way the whole play behaves. Their slipping through definitions, breaking down categories, refusing to let basic oppositions like male and female, losing and winning, fair and foul, truth and lies remain opposites, is merely the most extreme expression of the way the play as a whole works.

The witches are not an aberration, or a sideline. *Macbeth*, unlike *Hamlet* or *King Lear*, doesn't have sub-plots or digressions. It is, at a mere 2086 lines, remarkable for its compactness, its economy, the speed with which it moves. It is by far the shortest of Shakespeare's tragedies, so short that there is speculation that the version of *Macbeth* which we have may be itself an abridged one, shortened for performance at court. Either way, *Macbeth* is tightly written: the prominence that the witches have in it is strengthened by the shortness of the play as a whole. Shakespeare meant them to be as important in the overall structure as they still, inescapably, are. Some of the witches' lines (3, 5 and parts of 4, 1) are probably not by Shakespeare, but they are irrelevant ones. The witches, on the whole, are almost as central to the play as Macbeth himself.

From the start, the function of the witches is to confuse us and Macbeth. They are the first thing on stage and it is hard to say even what we see when we look at them. Are they natural or supernatural? If they are natural, are they female or male? We usually think of them as female because they are called the Weird Sisters: but it is by no means clear. The actors Shakespeare's own audience would have seen were men or possibly boys – women were not allowed to act on stage. The text tells us that they are also bearded. Banquo cannot decide: 'You should be women / And yet your beards forbid me to interpret / That you are so.' (1, 3, 43–44) And if they are not natural – again Banquo is unsure: They 'look not like the inhabitants o' th' earth / And yet are on't' (1, 3, 39–40) – are they real or just a delusion, a projection of some inner fantasy that Macbeth and Banquo have shared?

Theatrically, they are real enough – they are physically present on stage – but we can never be certain of the degree to which they are projecting the thoughts of those whom they encounter. The first thing Macbeth says in the play, for instance, – 'So foul and fair a day I have not seen' (1, 3, 36–) – is a direct echo of the witches – 'Fair is foul and foul is fair' (1, 1, 10) – almost, for a moment, as if this man whom we haven't seen before were just himself another of the witches. All of these things are consciously and deliberately left uncertain by Shakespeare, making the witches a running, living image of the loss of definition that is at the heart of the play.

2. Melting Gold

What is it that makes things so unstable, makes things turn into their opposites like this? For Shakespeare it is money. In another Shakespeare tragedy *Timon of Athens*, written around the same time as *Macbeth*, Timon talks of:

> Gold? Yellow, glittering, precious gold? . . .
> Thus much of this will make
> Black white, foul fair, wrong right,
> Base noble, old young, coward valiant . . .
> This yellow slave
> Will knit and break religions, bless th' accursed,
> Make the hoar leprosy ador'd, place thieves
> And give them title, knee and approbation,
> With senators on the bench . . . (4, 3, 26–)

It is money that makes foul fair and one of the earliest images in *Macbeth*, used twice in prominent places in the first three scenes, is of fair becoming foul and foul fair. Opposites are becoming interchangeable, categories are falling apart under the pressure of the rise of new money. One world view is slowly giving way to another, so that two overlapping worlds seem to exist at the same time, the world of order and duty on the one hand and the self-made world of men like Macbeth on the other. It is a frightening transition, one that desperately needs a ritual in which the blurred edges of the categories by which men and women understand their lives can be explored. Macbeth is such a ritual full of things and images that operate not naturalistically, not as a slice of real life, but ritualistically, as a way of calling up and exorcising this slippery, dangerous state.

Macbeth is a play that literally cannot be understood if it is approached with traditional tools like the analysis of character and the tragic flaw. Macbeth's flaw is the easiest of all to name. It is ambition: he tells us so himself. The problem is that when you look at the piece of the play where he talks about his ambition as dramatic action rather than as material for a report on his moral or psychological welfare, it is not so simple. In 1, 7, Macbeth names the compulsion he feels as 'ambition' but as soon as he gives it that name he rejects it. It is precisely when he calls himself ambitious that he is best able to decide not to kill Duncan ('We will proceed no further in this business'). He talks of ambition not as a positive reason for action but as something that is not sufficient to make him act:

> I have no spur to prick the sides of my intent, but only
> Vaulting ambition, which o'erleaps itself
> and falls on t'other –
> *Enter Lady Macbeth.* (1, 7, 25–)

Two things are to be noted about this speech. One is that it is left unfinished, cut off and rendered meaningless by the action. Lady Macbeth comes in and what follows are four lines, each of which ends with a question mark. The giving of a name to the thing that drives Macbeth is immediately undermined by a sequence of inconclusion and uncertainty. The second is that Macbeth's metaphor of mounting and spurring

135

horses is actually hopelessly confused. The metaphor of spurring – done when you are already on your horse – comes before the metaphor of mounting the horse. In other words the effect comes before the cause. To look to this speech which turns cause and effect on their heads for the cause of Macbeth's actions, the root of his character, is to look in the wrong place. Far from giving us the primary cause of what happens, the whole effect of the speech is to make a nonsense of cause and effect altogether.

If you look at what Shakespeare does with his sources for the story of *Macbeth*, the folly of looking for a simple motive for Macbeth's actions in the play becomes obvious. He uses two different stories from Holinshed's *Chronicles*, that of the mild and incompetent King Duncan killed by Macbeth and Banquo, and that of the murder of King Duff by Donwald, egged on by his wife. Now both of these killings have clear motives. In the first, Duncan is not particularly up to the job and Macbeth is in league with Banquo, making for a political coup d'état. In the second, Donwald kills King Duff as an act of revenge, part of a continuing blood-feud. But, although he follows the stories closely in other respects, Shakespeare is at pains to make sure that none of these motives remains in his version of the story: Duncan's stature is enhanced, his kindness to Macbeth emphasized. Banquo is set apart from the murder. Shakespeare, in fact goes to a lot of trouble to make the murder motiveless, to stop us from looking for a straightfor- ward personal motivation on Macbeth's part. The play is about many things but it is not about Macbeth's character and motives.

If it were, it wouldn't be very interesting. Viewed in isolation as a character, Macbeth is, at the most critical point of the play, merely a tool of his wife. The murder of Duncan is, in many ways, more her doing than his. What is most interesting about Macbeth, though, is not the clear connection between his 'character' and his actions, but the very lack of any such connection. There is in the play no relation between emotion and action – Macbeth does not hate or despise those he kills. He has no grudge against Duncan or Banquo, least of all against Lady Macduff and her children. Macduff, indeed, is the only person in the play who acts out of emotion – his hatred for Macbeth is real and fully motivated. Even the wronged Malcolm is cold and unemotional – everything we see or hear in the play emphasizes his lack of deep inner feeling.

Indeed one of the most splendidly ironic scenes in the play (3, 1) plays on this whole concern for motives. Macbeth is hiring the murderers to kill Banquo. They are professional killers and we have no interest in them beyond the function they have to perform. They have nothing to say, no glorious lines of poetry, no subtle distinctions of character. We are about as interested in them as we are in the motives of a mafia hit man: they do it for the money; that is all we know and all we need to know. And yet Macbeth insists on trying to supply them with a motive. Not content just to hire them to kill Banquo, he has to convince them – and in part himself – that they are repaying Banquo for past wrongs, that this is all part of a medieval revenge drama. He goes off on flights of rhetoric, more for their own sake than for any real effect on the murderers: when they look like joining in the game with the beginnings of a rhetorical answer, he cuts them off. Their response, for the most part, is perfunctory, but they recognize this as a charade they must go through, as a part of pleasing the customer:

> *Macbeth:* Both of you
>   Know Banquo was your enemy.
> *Murderers:* True, my lord. (3, 1, 115–)

If they were really stirred up by hatred and really convinced of the motive that Macbeth invents for them, they would launch into some formal expression of their emotions. But there is no railing, no denunciation, merely a 'True, my lord.' The scene shows us a world in which motives themselves have become inventions, a kind of formal fiction. It should be obvious that the play works from something else, from some other set of dramatic tensions.

3. Foetal Attractions

What *Macbeth* gives us instead is a struggle between Macbeth's desire to make his own destiny – the desire of the new world – and the rule-bound social order in which he lives. What is so powerful about *Macbeth* is the extent to which that struggle, in the play, is dramatized in ritual terms, through images of magic, of occult ceremonies, of witches, of unborn children. If Macbeth is a man in transition, then the things that speed him to his doom are the transitional things of rituals. The witches are half-human, half-otherworldly, their brew is full of those slippery, reptilian creatures that have altered significance because they are neither one thing nor the other, neither fish nor flesh, but slip between the categories: toads, snakes, newts, frogs, bats, adders, blindworms, lizards. And Macbeth, in his imagery, thinks of Banquo and Fleance the same way – he compares them to a snake and a worm (3, 2, 15 and 3, 4, 28) and connects them to the venom that the witches use in their brew (3, 4, 29). He also connects them in his mind to scorpions and bats (3, 2, 38 and 41). The linking of these half-and-half creatures to the dangers that Macbeth sees around him – Banquo and Fleance – an imagery that becomes real with the final assault on the castle by the half-men half-trees (Birnam Wood come to Dunsinane), is the dramatic medium by which the confusion of Shakespeare's own times is made concrete in the play.

The most powerful of these ritualistic images in the play, though, is that of the unborn child. In most traditional societies the unborn child is dangerously ambiguous and therefore of great ritual significance. The anthropologist Mary Douglas writes about the unborn child as belonging to the group of 'people who are somehow kept out of the patterning of society, who are placeless. They may be doing nothing wrong, but their status is indefinable . . . The unborn child's present position is ambiguous, its future equally so. For no one will say what sex it will have or whether it will survive the hazards of infancy. It is often treated as both unbearable and dangerous . . . Danger lies in transitional states, simply because transition is neither one state nor the next, it is indefinable.'

This notion that the unborn child was both dangerous and powerful – and therefore in need of being dealt with ritually – was a very live issue in Shakespeare's time. The belief that the unborn child was an evil spirit possessed by the devil had been the standard one, leading to the ceremony of baptism being conducted in conjunction with an exorcism of the child. At the church door the priest blew three times into the face of the child and said 'Go out of him unclean spirit, and give place to the Holy Ghost the comforter.' This practice had been officially dropped by the Protestants only in 1552 but it was still being hotly debated in Shakespeare's day with assertions such as that of the Vicar of Ashford, Kent, that unbaptized infants were the firebrands of Hell. The important point is that, in Shakespeare's world, the unborn child is recognized as supremely ambiguous, a powerful image of transition from one world to another, both innocent and dangerous, both vulnerable and powerful.

This is why images of unborn children run through *Macbeth*. Macbeth himself, by killing Duncan and rebelling against feudal order, makes himself one of those people who are left out of the patterning of society, who are placeless. He puts himself into the territory of the unborn children and they literally haunt him. In Lady Macbeth's shocking image (1, 7, 54–) the tenderness of the infant child turns to horrible violence:

> I would while it was smiling in my face,
> Have plucked my nipple from his boneless jaws
> And dashed the brains out . . .

Thereafter, unborn children, both dreadful and innocent, surround Macbeth. There is the witches':

> Finger of birth-strangled babe
> Ditch-delivered by a drab . . . (4, 1, 30–1)

which echoes Lady Macbeth's image. There is, most importantly, the line of unborn kings of Scotland, Banquo's unborn heirs, who are as central to the play as any living character because they dominate Macbeth's thoughts for most of the action. The 'bloody child' conjured on to the stage before us makes this danger to Macbeth physically present. And it links this line of unborn children to the other 'unborn child' who haunts Macbeth, Macduff. It is the 'bloody child' who tells Macbeth that 'none of woman born' will harm him. (4, 1, 96) Macduff is literally 'unborn', in the sense that the play quibbles on the word 'born' – he was not born in the conventional manner but by Caesarean section. And in his confrontation with Macbeth it is this that allows him to win out. Macbeth who has made himself like the unborn children – transitional, dangerous, yet curiously innocent, neither one thing nor the other – is eventually undone by them.

In this ritualized world, nothing will stay still. Good and bad, life and death, appearance and reality break out of their boundaries and turn into their opposites. Physically, the witches embody the spirit of Shakespeare's times: 'What seemed corporal melted / As breath into the wind' (1, 3, 81) and this description of them could be a motto for the whole play. Whereas in a fixed world, everything is divided into two – good and bad, life and death, male and female and so on – in *Macbeth* there is always a third that is neither one thing nor the other. In some cases, twos literally keep turning into threes. In Act 1, scene 7, Macbeth is musing on his 'double trust' towards Duncan, but this double becomes treble as he describes it: 'I am his kinsman and his subject . . . [and] his host.' Banquo's murderers, whom we meet as a pair, suddenly become, for no good reason, three (3, 3). The witches speak in three parts ('Show! / Show! / Show!'), show three apparitions, and make much of the number three ('Thrice the brinded cat hath mewed') – making Macbeth imagine he has three ears: 'Had I three ears I'd hear thee.' (4, 1, 94)

Right from the start, in fact, not only is fair foul and foul fair, but it is difficult to keep our minds on who is good and who is bad. We will learn, crudely, that Macbeth is evil and Banquo good, but before we meet them we have had them confused in our minds. The Captain's speeches (1, 2) and Duncan's questions make 'Macbeth' and 'Macbeth and Banquo' virtually interchangeable terms. More than this, the loyal Macbeth is virtually indistinguishable from the traitor Macdonwald. The latter is called 'merciless' but it is Macbeth whom we hear of as being merciless and the image is of them as 'two spent swimmers that do cling together'. Even in praising Macbeth and Banquo the Captain says it is as if 'they meant to memorize another Golgotha', associating them with the crucifiers of Christ, hardly a comforting image of goodness. We also have opposites, comfort and discomfort, being confused: 'whence comfort seems to come / Discomfort swells.' And then a traitor's name – Thane of Cawdor – being given to the greatest of the loyal soldiers, Macbeth. Hardly any wonder that the witches' chant of 'Double, double' is echoed here by the Captain – 'As cannons overcharged with double cracks / So they doubly redoubled strokes upon the foe.' (1, 2, 37–38) A basic description of the background to what will follow has become uncomfortably elusive, making what should be easy opposites, two sides in a battle, uneasy and shifty.

Simple things that shouldn't need defining at all become the subject of endless quibbling, of ifs and buts. We know, broadly speaking, what a man is, but in the slippery world of *Macbeth* it becomes hard to tell what a man is or isn't. Macbeth, having decided not to kill Duncan, maintains that anyone who would do so would cease to be a man:

> I dare do all that may become a man;
> Who dares do more is none. (1, 7, 46)

And he is right, for once he has killed Duncan, even the simple word 'man' starts to collapse and turn to nothing. At the beginning of the third act, one of the murderers, in conference with Macbeth about the plan to kill Banquo, utters the straightforward statement 'We are men, my liege.' (3, 1, 92) Macbeth refuses to accept the word 'man' as meaning anything and immediately launches into a tirade in which the murderers are compared to dogs and dogs themselves are split into their kinds and shapes.

Shortly afterwards, faced with the ghost of Banquo, Macbeth is caught by his own prophecy and ceases to be a man in the eyes of his wife, and indeed, of himself. She describes him as 'quite unmanned in folly' (3, 4, 73). She asks him 'Are you a man?' (3, 4, 59) and he casts doubt on the answer with his 'What man dare, I dare.' (3, 4, 100) When the ghost disappears, he says of himself that 'I am a man again' but the word has become so meaningless, so much a thing of nothing, that the statement, rather than restoring him to some fixed and well-defined state, serves only to mark the degree to which Macbeth himself has been cut adrift from recognizable limits.

And his disease is catching. In the next act, even his bitterest enemies start to sound like Macbeth on the subject of what a man is and does.

> *Malcolm:* Dispute it like a man.
> *Macduff:* But I must also feel it as a man. (4, 3, 221–)

As things fall apart, even the most basic of opposites, those of life and death, become fluid. As Macduff calls them to look at Duncan's murdered body, Malcolm and Banquo become ghosts rising from the dead, even though they are alive and well: 'As from your graves rise up and walk like sprites.' (2, 3, 78) Sleep becomes confused with death as 'death's counterfeit' (2, 3, 76), as 'the death of each day's life'. (2, 2, 36) The dead Banquo takes his place at Macbeth's supper and Macbeth wonders how it is that the dead will not stay dead: 'our graves must send / Those that we bury back . . .' (3, 4, 70–71) The sleepwalking Lady Macbeth (5, 1) is neither dead nor alive, but something in between. Malcolm and Macduff's cause, it is said, would 'excite the mortified man', that is, stir up the dead. (5, 2, 4) Macduff fears that 'my wife and children's ghosts will haunt me still.' (5, 8, 3) And again, Macbeth himself senses this loss of a clear distinction between life and death early on, knowing that the dead Duncan will still be 'alive' for himself, still shaping Macbeth's destiny and influencing everything that happens to him.

4. Fiddling the Prophets

If the relationship between cause and effect, between something that has happened in the past and something that exists in the present, is under stress in *Macbeth*, then so also is the relationship between the past and the future. This is the area of prophecy, and prophecy itself is a major concern of the play, as it was of Shakespeare's time. Prophecies, as we have seen, were taken seriously in Shakespeare's day, generally because they were a way of expressing the desire for political and social change, a desire that could not be expressed in any other language. The historian Keith Thomas makes this connection clear: 'It was the existence of rebellious feeling which led to the circulation of prophecies . . . It was rebels who read into them an application to current events, and they did so because they wished to do so. At times of stress, men scrutinized these ancient myths with a view to extracting from them some sanction for the dangerous courses of action upon which they proposed to embark. Under the pressure of change, they most felt the need for reassurance that what was happening had been foreseen by their ancestors and was in some sense part of

a larger plan. It was no accident that the periods when prophecies were most prominent in English life were precisely those of
rebellion, discontent and violent change . . . Prophecies disguised the break with the past.' This could be an exact
description of Macbeth, the violent rebel against the established order, and his relationship to the witches.

Not only prophecies but prophecies that lead to civil disorder and that boomerang on those who believe in them, were
constantly in the air in Shakespeare's time. No rebellion by
peasants and no treason trial was complete without reference
to the traitors and rebels being spurred on by false prophets.
And these prophecies were often bitterly ironic in exactly the
way that the witches' prophecies in *Macbeth* are, seeming to
offer victory but in fact foretelling disaster. Rebellious peasants
would go into battle at a certain place on foot of a prophecy
that that place would be filled with dead bodies, not realizing
that the dead bodies would be their own. In the year before
Macbeth was written, a gentleman could cite '26 ancient
Writers' in support of a prophecy that England would be torn
apart by religious wars. Two years earlier, the same prophecies
had been discussed by mourners at Queen Elizabeth's funeral.
Far from being an exotic fantasy, the whole theme of prophecy
in *Macbeth* is as topical to Shakespeare's audience as today's
headlines are to us, and just as threatening and dangerous.

The important point about the prophecies in the play is not
whether they are true or false, or whether Macbeth believes
them or not, but that they are both true and false, that
Macbeth both believes and does not believe them. Macbeth is
a man in transition, the play about a time of transition, and

that is why it is a tragedy. And one of the things that is changing in that transition is the belief in ancient wisdom and
prophecies. *Macbeth* is written in a century – the seventeenth –
at the beginning of which it is taken for granted that everything was known in the past and that wisdom has only to be
recovered, and at the end of which it is assumed that almost
nothing was known in the past and everything has to be
invented. Macbeth exists between one and the other, both
believing in the kind of system in which everything is already
known and can therefore be grasped by prophecy, and in the
opposite of that, a world in which everything, including yourself, has to be made up as you go along, in which precedent
and established order count for nothing.

Part of the tragic flaw idea of Macbeth is that he is unusu-
ally gullible, that he is too easily taken in by the witches,
implying that prophecy itself must self-evidently be nonsense.
But this is true neither to what we know of Macbeth himself
nor to the dramatic force of the play. The very first time we
hear of what Macbeth is like and what he does, it is the
Captain telling us of Macbeth 'Disdaining Fortune' (1, 2, 17),
that is, mocking preordained fate – the precise opposite of a
man who is overly inclined to believe prophecies that tell him
his fate has all been decided in advance. Even before Macbeth
meets the witches at all, there are disturbing prophecies spoken
unknowingly by others: Ross calls Macbeth 'Bellona's bride-
groom' (1, 2, 54), which is much truer than he thinks. Bellona
is the goddess of war, and Macbeth, as we will see, is in fact
married to a goddess of war, Lady Macbeth. Duncan gives
Macbeth, the soon-to-be traitor, the title of the traitorous

147

Thane of Cawdor. It is not in the first instance the devious witches who prophesy, but rather events and words spoken by others.

And this sense of unintentional prophecy continues throughout the play. Ross says that Macbeth being called Thane of Cawdor is 'an earnest of a greater honour' (1, 3, 102), which it turns out to be. It is the fact that he does become Thane of Cawdor that spurs Macbeth on to become king, which is indeed a greater honour, though not the one that Ross was thinking of. Macbeth's distracted conduct and rudeness towards Angus and Ross (1, 3) when they confirm a part of the witches' prophecy is itself a foreshadowing of the much more serious breach of civility and good manners in 3, 4 when Macbeth disrupts the supper on seeing the ghost of Banquo. Macduff's calling Banquo a ghost in 2, 3 is an unintentional prophecy of precisely what Banquo will be a few scenes later. In 4, 3, Macduff talks of 'welcome and unwelcome things at once' just before Ross comes in with the most unwelcome news imaginable – the slaughter of Macduff's wife and children. (Malcolm's tedious self-accusations in this scene, coming as they do after we have seen so many things spoken in one sense turning out to be true in another, increases our sense of foreboding about how Malcolm will rule. Why will Banquo's heirs succeed rather than Malcolm's? Will something of what Malcolm says about his own depravity turn out to be true?)

What this means is that in the play things do happen as predicted, even when the predictions are unintentional and have nothing at all to do with the witches. Prophecy not only operates independently of the witches, it is also not identified exclusively with evil. For Edward the Confessor, an image of pure goodness in the play, is said to have 'a heavenly gift of prophecy'. (4, 3, 158) It is therefore quite reasonable for Macbeth to believe in prophecy and it is the events of the play and not his 'character' which gives the prophecies their ironic weight.

It is important to remember that if Macbeth fully believed the witches' prophecies, there would be no tragedy. If he was a superstitious medieval man, he would take these supernatural portents at face value and assume, as he is tempted to do, that the prophecies will fulfil themselves without his having to take any action at all:

> If chance will have me King, why, chance may crown
>   me,
> Without my stir. (1, 3, 143–)

It would be pointless to kill Duncan, and even more pointless to kill Banquo, in an attempt to frustrate the second part of the prophecy. If, on the other hand, he were a modern rational man, he would discount the prophecies as gibberish or, as the Puritans of Shakespeare's time would have done, as the work of the devil. But he is neither one thing nor the other. Like a modern man he sees himself as the maker of his own fate. Like a medieval man, he is profoundly affected by the prophecies. He believes them when they tell him what he wants to hear, and disbelieves them when they do not. At the very moment when he is most in thrall to them – plotting the murder of Banquo because of them – he also announces his defiance of fate, of the notion of a pre-ordained future: 'come, fate, into the list'. (3, 1, 72) He is destroyed by being caught in the middle between two systems of belief.

It is significant that the individuals who haunt Macbeth by way of the witches' prophecies are themselves split and divided. He fears both Banquo and Fleance; he attacks both Macduff and Macduff's family. And the actions he takes on foot of the prophecies are both double and doubly ironic. He gives the Murderers a double task: to kill Banquo and to kill Fleance, and they carry out half of it. He sets out to kill Macduff and Macduff's family, and he achieves half of it. And in each case it is the wrong half. If he is to act on the prophecies, then he needs to kill Fleance and Macduff. What he manages to do is to kill Fleance's father, Banquo, and Macduff's son; the wrong father and the wrong son. The whole thing balances out neatly – he kills a father and a son – but the neatness is grotesquely wrong.

And this is one of the most remarkable things about *Macbeth*. We expect a tragedy – think, for instance, of *King Lear* or *Hamlet* – to end in chaos, with everything in a mess, having fallen apart more or less completely. If there is terror in these plays, it is in the utter disorder of things. But *Macbeth* works differently. What is terrifying at the end of *Macbeth* is not how disorderly things are but how orderly. Everything, especially those things which seemed impossible, fits together neatly. Birnam Wood does come to Dunsinane. Macduff is not of woman born.

In this, *Macbeth* is the closest of Shakespeare's plays to the old Greek tragedies with which his work is often, wrongly, compared. The sense of a prophecy being fulfilled in unexpected ways, of a coincidence that is disturbing because it is too neat is like that of *Oedipus Rex*, where the hero discovers that by a grotesque string of coincidences and in fulfilment of a prophecy, he has married his own mother. In *Macbeth*, Shakespeare, like Sophocles before him, plays on something that we know from our daily lives: that coincidences, things fitting together too neatly, far from being orderly and comforting, are deeply disturbing because they remind us of disorder. When things fit together purely by chance, as they do in *Macbeth* and in the coincidences of our daily lives, they remind us of how powerful chance is, of how even the most unlikely things are likely to happen. Far from convincing us that there is a pattern and an order to everything, coincidences make us feel that everything is random, that meaning and significance occur only through a meaningless accident.

This is the sense that we get at the end of the play. The neatness of everything arises out of the meaninglessness and disorder that are all around. We have just heard from Macbeth in the 'Tomorrow, and tomorrow, and tomorrow' speech (5, 5, 17–) one of the most powerful evocations of meaninglessness in all of literature. The whole state of Scotland is in chaos. Foul whisperings, as the Doctor says, are abroad. The order of nature itself has been upset. And then here we have this neat, orderly ending. The neatness is deliberately perverse, for it serves really to underline the absurdity of everything else.

For instance, the meaninglessness of Macbeth's death, and that of Lady Macbeth, is stressed by the neatness with which the death of Young Siward (5, 8) is rounded-off by being discussed, commented on and polished with the regulation words of praise. But this piece of neatness, this conventional tidying up, is in fact disturbingly out of place. We don't actually give a damn about Young Siward. He has appeared for at most two minutes in the fifth act, where his sole function has been as an adjunct to Macbeth, a necessary piece of stage furniture so that we can see Macbeth being defiant, fierce, his old military self again for a few minutes before his death. By neatly tying up Young Siward's death, Shakespeare stresses how appallingly casual have been the deaths of the two most interesting characters, for the audience, in the play – Macbeth and Lady Macbeth. It is neatness and order used to make us aware of disorder and chaos, in the same way that the neat coincidence of the witches' prophecies being fulfilled at the end serves not to make us satisfied at the symmetry of the conclusion but to leave us disturbed and disconcerted.

The significant thing about all of this is that it makes us feel uncomfortable about order, pattern, things being in their proper place. Macbeth needing to kill a father and a son but killing the wrong father and the wrong son, the proper forms of marking a death being gone through but for the wrong character, the prophecies working out but in bizarre and unpredictable ways, all serve to undermine the whole idea of order itself. So while the things that happen in the play – the traitor being punished and the rightful succession to the throne being re-established – serve to uphold the values of order, duty and the proper patterns of feudal society, the way they happen serves to subvert those very values. This is the dramatic tension which is at the heart of the play, and it is because Macbeth is the focus for that tension that he is so interesting and so exciting. He contains within himself not just a 'character' but a whole set of conflicts that embody a society and a history.

Another way to get at this tension is through looking at Malcolm. Malcolm is the embodiment of the order that is to be restored, the play's location of active goodness. But there is an enormous tension for anyone watching the play between what we know about Malcolm and what we feel about him, between what he says and the way he says it. We know that he is good, but we feel that he is boring. We agree with what he says but wish he would either get on with it or say it with even a little of the poetic force Macbeth can manage. Morally, we are on his side, dramatically we are against him. We want him to win, but we don't want to have to listen to him. His 'Oh, by whom?' on hearing of the death of his royal and beloved father writes him off as a man of emotional depth.

In 4, 3 he bores us to tears with his long-winded game of self-accusation, and this irritation on our part is clearly what Shakespeare intends. The scene is placed in such a way, immediately after the murder of Macduff's family, as to heighten its dull coyness when compared to the heart-stopping and heart-rending action we have just witnessed. We know what Macduff does not yet know and to see Malcolm tease him and torture him with his verbal game can only make Malcolm not merely boring but somewhat despicable in our eyes. And the quality of Malcolm's response to Macduff's grief can only reinforce this negative impression of him. It is as bad as his 'Oh, by whom?', with Malcolm stupidly urging a stiff upper lip on a man whose life has just collapsed, offering no real human sympathy and attempting repeatedly to turn Macduff's pain to his own military purposes. Macduff's line 'He has no children' (4, 3, 217) is often taken as referring to Macbeth (thus giving rise to pointless arguments about how many children Lady Macbeth has) but it is far more likely that it is directed at Malcolm, a bitter put-down of the latter's shallow and insensitive pretence at knowing how to 'cure this deadly grief'.

Macbeth moves quickly and feels deeply; Malcolm moves slowly and has no capacity for deep feeling whatsoever. Even in the numerical symbolism of the play, it is noticeable that Malcolm is a lesser figure than Macbeth. Macbeth's twos become threes (his 'double trust', three murderers and three ears, mentioned earlier), but Malcolm's twos become one. At the start of the play, he is part of a duo, seen always in tandem with his brother Donalbain. At the end of the play, he is, inexplicably, one – Donalbain, for some unknown reason, has disappeared. In more than one sense we get the disturbing feeling that Malcolm has something missing.

With all this in mind it is particularly eerie that Malcolm's final speech, the one in which order is restored and the action is tied up, is almost an exact echo of Duncan's speech near the beginning of the play when the earlier battle is concluded, the succession to the throne is settled, a traitor is beheaded (Macdonwald), rewards are promised and titles are given out. Malcolm speaks his last speech with a battle won, the succession to the throne settled, a traitor beheaded (Macduff has just come in with Macbeth's head) and in it he promises rewards and distributes titles. And we know what happened after Duncan's speech – instead of being a prelude to peace, order and a smooth handing-on of the crown, it was a prelude to treason, disorder and the seizing of the crown by Macbeth. Two things combine to make this echo eerie. One is the fact that throughout the play, we have seen things being foreshadowed in all sorts of unintentional ways, and we are by now used to the idea of accidental prophecies. The other is that the idea of an ending itself is one of the things that have been consistently denied throughout the play.

Early in the play (1, 7, 1–), Macbeth devotes a whole speech ('If it were done when 'tis done, then 'twere well / It were done quickly') to the question of whether an action can ever be finished. The speech is interrupted by Lady Macbeth and is itself left unfinished. It is also the beginning of a set of actions – the murder of Duncan – whose consequences will never be done with for Macbeth. The murder itself refuses to be finished in one go – Lady Macbeth has to go back with the knives. Duncan's blood will not wash off. The days will not end in sleep. Banquo refuses to die in two ways – he comes back as a ghost and he lives on, in a sense, in his children who will be kings hereafter. Macbeth cannot say 'Amen', the word which finishes a prayer. (2, 2, 29) Macduff fears that his wife and children, though dead, will come back to haunt him if he does not revenge himself on Macbeth. Far from being given reason to believe that the end of the play is the end of the story, our experience in watching the play is that things refuse to end at all.

The point in all of this is that *Macbeth* is not a play which merely shows that order is good and disorder is bad. The order that is restored at the end of the play and the formal orderliness of the prophecies turning out to be true, are, respectively, weak and disturbing. Vicious, destructive and obsessive as he may be, Macbeth exists within an order that offers little in the way of a convincing alternative to him. Shakespeare shows us the cost of the disorder which Macbeth unleashes – the murders of innocent people, the ruin of Scotland – but also, in a sense, its necessity. It is not for nothing that Macbeth, through his use of the witches' prophecies, is identified with the social rebels of Shakespeare's time, with their inevitable but inevitably doomed rebellions. Like them, he is caught in a time of disturbing change in which he can do little except rebel. Like them, too, he cannot win. He is forced into an act which is out of its place in history, into a desire for which there is no possible fulfilment.

5. The Big World

How does Macbeth, who is in many ways so appalling a figure, come to be someone who can seem to represent, not just himself, but a whole human dilemma and a whole sense of history? Surely we would prefer to see him as an isolated madman, which is what he has become by the end of the play, than to take him as representing us and, in certain moments, speaking for us. The answer is that we would prefer to do just this, but the play does not let us do so. It is partly that, as we have mentioned, the alternatives to Macbeth in the play – Duncan, Banquo, Malcolm – are so bland and so boring that they make his passion, speed and awareness of himself all the more attractive.

The one passionate and strong alternative to Macbeth, Macduff, is temperamentally inclined to keep out of nasty situations – he absents himself from Macbeth's coronation and isn't around when the murderers come for his family – and is stirred to vigorous action only by hatred and the desire for revenge. He acts out of an immediate and personal cause, whereas Macbeth is impelled to go against his personal instincts and engage himself with things that are so big and general that they are impossible for him to pin down: the future, the supernatural, the forces that control human destiny. Macduff operates in a small world, Macbeth, for all his obsessive violence, operates in a very big one.

For what Macbeth is concerned about more than anything else is the future, and this is what is really remarkable about him. Most of us live day by day and think of the future, if at all, only occasionally and in the abstract. It is not, to us, real. Macbeth's curse is that it is real for him, often more real than the present. The witches give him a little taste of the future and it becomes addictive. As the play goes on, it becomes more and more important to him, blotting out the present almost completely. His present life, his achievement of the position of King of Scotland, is of no consequence to him. What he craves is to control the future, to be the father of kings who will rule long after he is dead. The obsession reaches such a point that when something immediate and dramatic happens to him in the present – the death of Lady Macbeth – he immediately wishes it were part of the future:

'She should have died hereafter'. (5, 5, 17) Lady Macbeth set out to feel the future in the present ('I feel now / The future in the instant', 1, 5, 56), but in the end Macbeth's feelings for her are obliterated by the future and his obsession with it.

Why does this sense of the future take such a hold over Macbeth? The reasons have to do with his sense of his own time in history. He kicks against his own time and its values of order and hierarchy and duty. He wants to be free to act on his desires, though he has no concrete sense of what those desires really are. But he knows, too, that he cannot do this in the present, that the time and the place in which he lives simply don't work like that. So what he wants is to live in a future time. He wants to control the future by being the father of its rulers. He wants, in a sense, to be his own descendants. This is why it is much more important to him that he succeed in killing Fleance than it was to kill Duncan. The present – being king – matters only as a stepping stone to the future. It is important to be king not in itself but because only a king can found a dynasty which will control the future.

This, too, is the reason why time haunts him so much. Time runs through the play like a seam of ore. The second act begins with Banquo asking Fleance what time it is, and is punctuated by a kind of ticking clock – the bell rings to signal that it is time for the killing of Duncan and rings again when the crime is discovered. Then time starts to go wrong. It is day by the clock, says Ross, (2, 4, 6–7) and yet 'dark night strangles the travelling lamp'. From now on, time gets in everywhere and is spoken of as an actor in the drama itself, a force that has been let loose: 'fill up the time', 'let every man be the master of his

158

time', 'the perfect spy o' th' time', 'the pleasure of the time', the 'last syllable of recorded time'. The last speech of the play uses the word 'time' three times, and, remarkably, when Macduff holds up the head of Macbeth, he doesn't say 'Scotland is free' or 'We are free', but 'The time is free.' (5, 11, 21)

And the line makes sense. For Macbeth's obsession with the future, his desire to make himself part of some other time than his own, has been an attempt to capture time and bring it under his command. When he can't do this, he tries to destroy time altogether. Like all tyrants, he wants to destroy what he cannot control. His own reaction to Lady Macbeth's death brings home to him his failure to control the future, for in spite of his desire that she should have died in the future, she hasn't done so. So he conjures up a vision in which time is obliterated, in which one day becomes the same as the next, and therefore there is no such thing as past, present and future. All three are meshed together in one meaningless whole:

> To-morrow, and to-morrow, and to-morrow
> Creeps in this petty pace from day to day
> To the last syllable of recorded time . . . (5, 5, 19–)

But, and this is the other main reason why the play does not permit us to distance ourselves from Macbeth, his vain and hopeless desire to live in the future, to be alive in a time where he would not be trapped by the rules of history and the confines of his own time's values, is something that we all, in some sense, share. Because there has never been a perfect world, a world that would match our desires, and because we all dream sometime that such a world might exist in the future, we share his attraction to that future. Like the peasants of Shakespeare's time who revolted against the order of the day and cited prophecies as their excuse, Macbeth is a rebel whose cause can only make sense long after he is dead. That is his tragedy and also, to a degree, ours.

It is Macbeth's great speeches that make this connection between us and him, for, in spite of surface appearances, they are not the purely private, inner thoughts of an isolated man. Indeed, one of the most extraordinary things that Shakespeare does in the play is to break down the whole notion of what is internal and what is external. In the early part of the play, the difference between our inner selves (our hearts) and our outer, public selves (our faces) is a major concern of the imagery: 'There's no art / To find the mind's construction in the face.'; 'look like th' innocent flower, / But be the serpent under't.'; 'False face must hide what the false heart doth know.' When so many other differences – between fair and foul, truth and lies, men and women – are breaking down, this is the difference that is insisted on – between what we are inside and what we look like to other people.

But it is a distinction that is set up so clearly only to be knocked down all the more forcefully. *Macbeth* is indeed full of soliloquies – fifteen per cent of it is monologue, as compared with just eight per cent of *Hamlet* – and Macbeth does become very obviously isolated, as he tells us himself in 'My way of life / Is fall'n into the sear, the yellow leaf . . .' But there is nothing private or internal about these soliloquies. Instead, Shakespeare

160

develops a way of speaking in which there is no distinction between the internal thoughts and feelings of a character and the outward expression of these feelings, or where at the very least that distinction is made unclear. We are made used to this kind of speech in two scenes: that of Banquo's ghost and the sleepwalking scene.

The words that Macbeth speaks to Banquo's Ghost in 3, 4 are both internal speech and external speech. From the point of view of everyone but Macbeth, they are a soliloquy – a man talking to himself, expressing his inner thoughts. Because they cannot see the Ghost, they cannot see that he is addressing those words to someone in particular. But from the point of view of Macbeth, these words are not soliloquy but dialogue: they are addressed directly to the Ghost and expect an answer. Thus they are at one and the same time inner and outer, demolishing the distinction between these two which has been so carefully established earlier.

This is taken, if anything, further in the sleepwalking scene, where Lady Macbeth's private, internal thoughts, so private that she is not herself even conscious of saying them out, are overheard and discussed by the Doctor and the Waiting Woman. They are even written down and recorded by the Doctor.

And almost immediately after this scene we have Macbeth speaking out his most private thoughts, again overheard by the Doctor. The soliloquy at 5, 3, 22– ('My way of life etc.') which is more nakedly self-revealing and self-critical than any in the play is not properly speaking a soliloquy at all, for it is spoken before an on-stage audience. We could call it public speech, except that by now the distinction between what is public and what is private has completely disappeared. And this is followed by the 'To-morrow, and to-morrow, and to-morrow' speech, which takes the process to its final point.

Surrounded by his soldiers and his battle flags, Macbeth gives expression to his deepest internal feelings, his most profoundly personal sentiments. But he does not use the word 'I' or talk about himself. He uses the word 'our' and talks about humanity. His vision of humanity may come out of his personal situation, it may be bleak, but the humanity which he speaks of is still a common humanity. And there is no longer the possibility of deceit. The heart can now be read in the face, the mind's construction emerges directly in the spoken word. What was not possible at the beginning of the play – to know what someone thinks and feels from what they say and do – has become not only possible, but unavoidable. For at least one moment in time, a man's inner self is not denied and refuted by the external world of history and power and violence. It is a moment that cannot last and that is quickly swallowed up by the forces of power and order and the values of Macbeth's own time, represented by Macduff and Malcolm and their troops. If we are glad to see Macbeth go, we are also glad to have had that moment.

Acknowledgements

Every year about one thousand books and articles on Shakespeare are published. As I read hardly any of them, I do not know how much, if any, of this book is really original. I do know, however, that I have borrowed to a greater or lesser extent from a number of writers, and I would like to acknowledge this debt.

Relatively little of what I have used is from literary critics, but one book, Stephen Booth's brilliant *King Lear, Macbeth, Indefinition, and Tragedy* (Yale University Press, 1983) is a big influence on the chapters on *Lear* and *Macbeth* here. I have taken much from Booth's readings of those plays, though the use I make of those readings is, for better or worse, my own. The work of Raymond Williams, too, is an important element in the discussion of soliloquies here.

The work of three historians is also an important influence. Keith Thomas's *Religion and the Decline of Magic* (Peregrine

Books, 1978) provides much of the historical context and detail. Robert Darnton's essay 'Philosophers Trim the Tree of Knowledge' (in *The Great Cat Massacre*, Peregrine Books, 1985) is used in my discussion of ritual and changing categorizations of knowledge. Philippe Aries's *The Hour of Our Death* (Peregrine Books, 1983) has a bearing on the discussion of ideas of death in the chapter on *Hamlet*.

The idea of seeing Shakespeare's tragedies as a kind of ritual is at least partly suggested by John Holloway's *The Story of the Night* (Routledge and Kegan Paul, 1961). The elaboration of that idea here owes much to the work of the anthropologist Mary Douglas in *Purity and Danger* (Ark Paperbacks, 1984).

The work of a number of theatre directors has also been important in formulating these ideas, even if only as something to react against. Grigori Kozintsev's *Shakespeare: Time and Conscience* (Dobson Books, 1967) has long been a source of inspiration, and the essay on *King Lear* here follows its spirit. I have also used occasional ideas from Jonathan Miller's *Subsequent Performances* (Faber and Faber, 1986), Peter Brook's *The Shifting Point* (Methuen, 1984) and Charles Marowitz's Introduction to *The Marowitz Hamlet* (Penguin Plays, 1970).

Finally, there are a number of individuals who bear much of the credit and none of the blame for this book. Brendan Flynn and his students at Clifden Community School both inspired the idea of the book and suffered its earliest fumblings. Dermot Bolger, Neil Belton and Angela Rose have provided encouragement, sustenance, and the necessary threats. Colm Tóibín's comments and criticisms have been invaluable. And Clare Connell has been, as always, indispensable.